NATIONAL GEOGRAPHIC
KiDS

BITE, STING, KILL!

THE INCREDIBLE SCIENCE OF TOXINS, VENOM, FANGS & STINGERS

JULIE BEER

NATIONAL GEOGRAPHIC
WASHINGTON, D.C.

CONTENTS

INTRODUCTION

WATCH YOUR STEP! YOU ARE ABOUT TO EXPLORE THE WORLD'S MOST DEADLY CREATURES. They're in the air and they're buried underground. They're floating in the sea and they're hidden deep in underwater caves. They're in deserts and tropical forests. They're in your backyard. They may even be in your house! Some bite with razor-sharp fangs; others sting at lightning speed with their tails. There are even some that stun by a simple touch.

We're talking about venomous animals, and no matter how they deliver their toxins, they pack a serious punch! Venomous reptiles, invertebrates, marine animals, and mammals live on land and in the sea and air around the world. Most have little interest in doing humans the slightest harm. But if you're a predator looking to attack or an item on their dinner menu, watch out! It's a critter-eat-critter world, and these critters have lethal bites!

Turn the page and find out what all the buzz is about!

REPTILES THAT STRIKE

THESE VENOMOUS ANIMALS HAVE A VICIOUS BITE

A VENOMOUS LIZARD THE SIZE OF A SMALL CAR. A snake capable of taking down an elephant. A "monster" that sends venom into its victims while it's chewing on them. Sound like the makings of the ultimate thriller movie? It's real life. And it's just the beginning.

For the most part, reptiles are unassuming and would much rather avoid people and carry on with their day. But a handful of lizards and about 600 of the world's 3,000 snake species are venomous—they have saliva that carries toxins, also known as venom. Some are mildly venomous—packing just enough to kill a small animal, like a mouse. Others are so dangerous they should hold a caution sign.

Get ready to find out about a snake that "stands up" taller than you, a lizard that can kill with the germs in its mouth, and a group of professionals who spend their days collecting venom from some of the world's deadliest creatures.

VENOMOUS SNAKES can be found on every continent except Antarctica.

BLACK MAMBA

SHY, FAST, AND DEADLY

The black mamba is **ONE OF THE MOST FEARED SNAKES IN SUB-SAHARAN AFRICA**—and for good reason: It can reach lengths of up to 14 feet (4.3 m) and is one of the fastest snakes in the world, slithering up to 12.5 miles an hour (20 km/h)—that's faster than an average kid can sprint! But their size and speed aren't what gives black mambas their fearsome reputation—their fangs are.

Black mambas sometimes sleep in empty TERMITE MOUNDS.

THE BITE

Black mambas are widely considered the **WORLD'S DEADLIEST SNAKE.** Just a few drops of their venom are enough to kill a human, and they don't just bite once—they'll **STRIKE REPEATEDLY.** To be fair though, they do give a warning: When agitated by a potential predator—whether it's a human or mongoose threatening to steal its eggs—a black mamba raises its head, lifts up to a third of its body off the ground, spreads the "hood" of its neck, and opens its mouth wide for an intimidating hiss.

Black mambas also strike to get their meals, which mostly include small mammals such as squirrels and other rodents. That's when their venom comes in.

BLACK MAMBAS AREN'T BLACK! They are olive-gray, but the inside of their mouths is all black.

☠ THE KILL

WHEN IT BITES, a black mamba's **VENOM GOES INTO ITS PREY'S BLOODSTREAM,** attacking both the nervous system—which sends messages from the brain and spinal cord to other parts of the body—and heart. The snake waits for the venom to paralyze the animal and then begins to swallow it. Before there was medication (called antivenom) to treat venomous bites, **IT MEANT CERTAIN DEATH IF A PERSON WAS BITTEN** by a black mamba, and in rural areas that don't have hospitals or antivenom available, the snakes still pose a risk. The good news: If medicine is given quickly, bite victims can make a full recovery.

AT A GLANCE

SCIENTIFIC NAME:
Dendroaspis polylepis

SIZE:
Up to 14 feet (4.3 m) long

HABITAT:
Savannas and rocky hills

A **BLACK MAMBA'S** head is shaped like a coffin.

KOMODO DRAGON

A GIANT LIZARD WITH A VICIOUS BITE

IMAGINE A VENOMOUS 300-POUND (136-KG) LIZARD that's as long as a small car and wields serrated teeth like a bread knife. Sound like a prehistoric creature from the Jurassic period? Believe it or not, it's living on Earth right now, wandering around a small group of islands in Indonesia.

When threatened, Komodo dragons sometimes INTENTIONALLY THROW UP to make themselves lighter for a quick getaway.

 THE BITE

THE KOMODO DRAGON WILL EAT JUST ABOUT ANYTHING—FROM DEER TO PIGS TO WATER BUFFALO—EVEN HUMANS, IN RARE INSTANCES. It's big and scaly with a huge powerful tail, and generally doesn't move particularly fast (although it can, if it has to). Its main method of snatching prey is an exercise in patience. It hunkers down and waits for prey to pass by, then springs into action, using its shark-like teeth to take a bite.

☠ THE KILL

KOMODO DRAGONS RELEASE A TYPE OF VENOM THAT LOWERS BLOOD PRESSURE AND CAUSES MASSIVE BLEEDING. If the prey manages to escape after it's been bitten, it likely won't be free for long. Once the venom sets in (and it can take a while), the dragon will use its specialized sense of smell to track down the bitten prey. **KOMODO DRAGONS HAVE BEEN KNOWN TO FOLLOW WOUNDED PREY FOR MILES!** Once they do catch up with their victim, they feast. They are capable of eating 80 percent of their body weight in a single feeding.

A Komodo dragon can smell **ROTTING FLESH** 2.5 miles (4 km) away.

AT A GLANCE

SCIENTIFIC NAME:
Varanus komodoensis

SIZE:
10 feet (3 m) long;
300 pounds (136 kg)

HABITAT:
Tropical savanna forests

WHERE'S THE TOOTHBRUSH?

A Komodo dragon's mouth is a germy place.
Its serrated teeth tear into the flesh of its prey like a bread knife, and then the flesh gets stuck in its jagged teeth, producing lots of bacteria. The bacteria spread to their saliva, so when the dragon bites into an animal, the bacteria transfer to the wound. If a Komodo dragon's prey isn't killed by the dragon's deadly venom, it'll soon face a nasty—and probably life-threatening—infection.

13

WHITE-LIPPED GREEN PIT VIPER

A SNAKE WITH A SUPER SENSE

The white-lipped green pit viper, one of about 190 pit viper species and found throughout Southeast Asia, has a good sense about where to find its next meal. **THE SNAKE HAS TWO "PITS," ONE ON EACH SIDE OF ITS HEAD BETWEEN EACH EYE AND NOSTRIL.** The pits are actually organs that sense the heat given off by warm-blooded prey. The snake processes this information in the same part of the brain that it uses to see, which gives it a **THERMAL IMAGE TO AIM AND STRIKE** at, even in pitch darkness!

Unlike its green relatives, Indonesia's white-lipped island pit viper is **BRIGHT BLUE.**

 THE BITE

Heat sensing isn't the white-lipped green pit viper's only superpower. Like all vipers, it also has **HINGED FANGS THAT POP OUT FROM THE ROOF OF ITS MOUTH** when it opens wide. These clamp down on its prey, including small birds, frogs, and rodents.

☠ THE KILL

PIT VIPER FANGS DELIVER VENOM THAT BREAKS DOWN AND DESTROYS BLOOD VESSELS IN THEIR VICTIM, LEADING TO INTERNAL BLEEDING. Unlike other venomous snakes that release their prey after they strike, pit vipers hold on tight. They have **FLEXIBLE JAWS THAT THEY USE TO "WALK" LARGE PREY INTO THEIR MOUTHS, WHOLE.** In the islands of Indonesia, human contact with white-lipped green pit vipers is fairly common—leading to as many as 50 percent of all venomous bites humans experience, although death is rare.

A new species of pit viper was given the name Salazar pit viper after the Harry Potter character SALAZAR SLYTHERIN, one of the magical school's founders.

AT A GLANCE

SCIENTIFIC NAME:
Cryptelytrops albolabris

SIZE:
Up to three feet (90 cm) long

HABITAT:
Shrubland and forests

LISSSTEN FOR THE HISS

White-lipped green pit vipers are fearsome predators of small animals, but the white-lipped's cousin, the saw-scaled viper, is a greater threat to humans. When agitated, the snake forms into S-shaped folds, and when its scales rub against each other, they produce a cautionary hissing sound. Don't dismiss the hiss! Saw-scaled snakes have one of the fastest strikes, and their venom is powerful. Found in Africa, the Middle East, and central Asia (including India), saw-scaled snakes are responsible for about 5,000 human deaths per year—more than any other kind of snake worldwide.

SNAKE FANGS

HOW DO THEY WORK?

FROM ITS FORKED TONGUE TO ITS SERIOUS HISS, A SNAKE HAS PLENTY OF SIGNATURE FEATURES. But one snake trait commands the most respect: the fangs.

Venomous snakes use their fangs to inject venom into their prey, but not all snake fangs are the same. Some snake species have fangs that are hollow—like a needle that delivers a vaccine. That's the case with the Gaboon viper, which has the world's longest snake fangs. They're up to two inches (5 cm) long—that's as long as two paper clips lined up end to end! The venom travels through the fangs and is injected into prey. Other species have solid fangs in the back of their mouths that have grooves in them to channel venom.

Snake venom is actually a type of saliva (or spit) made by special glands located behind a snake's eyes. Some snakes' venom is harmless to people, but others can be very toxic. There are three general groups of snake venom: hemo-toxins, cytotoxins, and neurotoxins—and they each work in a different way. Some snake species deliver just one type of venom and others deliver a combi-nation. Regardless, each type of venom can mean big trouble for a snake's prey.

◄ **HEMOTOXINS** Common in vipers and pit vipers, this venom attacks the prey's blood. Some varieties prevent blood clotting, which causes uncontrollable bleeding until the prey dies. Other varieties speed up blood clotting.

▼ **CYTOTOXINS** Found in American rattlesnakes, this type of venom destroys cells, usually in muscles, and causes tissue to break down. This makes it easier for prey to be swallowed.

◄ **NEUROTOXINS** Common in cobras, coral snakes, and sea snakes, this venom blocks or destroys parts of the prey's nervous system—the system in the body that sends signals. This type of venom can cause prey to become paralyzed, stop breathing, or collapse.

17

GILA MONSTER

CHEW YOUR FOOD!

WITH A NAME LIKE "GILA MONSTER," YOU MIGHT ASSUME THIS REPTILE MEANS BIG TROUBLE. Sure, it's the largest venomous lizard in the U.S., making its home in deserts in the Southwest, and **IT'S COVERED IN AN ARMOR OF BEAD-LIKE SCALES.** But its venom is only a serious threat to its small animal prey—and any predators who dare to attack.

🦷 THE BITE

The Gila (pronounced HEE-luh) monster **DOESN'T ATTACK ITS PREY WITH A STRIKE—IT GOES STRAIGHT TO CHEWING.** Unlike other venomous animals—such as snakes and spiders—that inject their venom, the Gila monster latches on to its prey and begins to chew. That's when the monster's neurotoxins move through grooves in its teeth and seep into its prey's open wounds.

☠ THE KILL

GILA MONSTERS ARE SLOW MOVERS. THEY MOSTLY EAT BABY MAMMALS THAT CAN'T QUICKLY ESCAPE, OR THEY STEAL EGGS FROM NESTS—sometimes high up in cactuses. While a Gila monster's chomp is painful for humans, its venom isn't toxic enough to kill, and it would be pretty easy to outrun if you ever did cross paths with one. They are not large, at about two feet (0.6 m) long, but are hard to spot because they live almost their entire lives in underground burrows. Their motivation to come aboveground is to soak up the sun or eat. Gila monsters store fat in their tails and can go for long periods of time without a meal.

A Gila monster's **TOP RUNNING SPEED** is only 1.5 miles an hour (2.4 km/h).

AT A GLANCE

SCIENTIFIC NAME:
Heloderma suspectum

SIZE:
20 inches (51 cm)

HABITAT:
Deserts

Gila monsters can eat as few as **THREE BIG MEALS A YEAR.**

KING COBRA

A SNAKE WITH A ROYAL PRESENCE

If a snake can "stand up" tall enough to look a grown person in the eye, it deserves a crown. **MEASURING UP TO 18 FEET (5.5 M), THE KING COBRA IS THE WORLD'S LONGEST VENOMOUS SNAKE.** When faced with a threat, it raises a third of its body up off the ground and starts slithering forward. Not intimidating enough? **IT ALSO FLARES OUT ITS "HOOD," A FLAP OF SKIN BEHIND ITS HEAD, AND LETS OUT A LOW HISS THAT SOUNDS LIKE A GROWL.**

Male king cobras sometimes **WRESTLE EACH OTHER** to compete for females.

THE BITE

King cobras, which live in the forests and plains of India, southern China, and Southeast Asia, can be found on land, in water, and in trees. **THEIR FAVORITE MEAL OF CHOICE? OTHER SNAKES.** They are resistant to the venom of all their prey. They're cannibals, too—they'll eat other king cobras. **KING COBRAS HAVE HALF-INCH (1.3-CM)-LONG TEETH** that are angled backward, allowing them to push their prey toward their stomachs.

20

☠ THE KILL

A KING COBRA'S VENOM IS A NEURO-TOXIN—THAT MEANS IT SHUTS DOWN ITS PREY'S BREATHING SYSTEM AFTER IT STRIKES. Drop for drop, a king cobra's venom is not as potent as other snakes', but it releases a lot of venom with each bite— **ONE BITE IS ENOUGH TO KILL AN ELEPHANT!**

King cobras are the only snakes that **BUILD NESTS** for their eggs.

AT A GLANCE

SCIENTIFIC NAME:
Ophiophagus hannah

SIZE:
Up to 18 feet (5.5 m) long

HABITAT:
Rainforests and plains

AIM FOR THE EYES

SPITTING COBRAS HIT WHERE IT COUNTS

VENOMOUS SNAKES' GREATEST WEAPONS ARE USUALLY THEIR FANGS, BUT IN THE CASE OF SPITTING COBRAS, IT'S THEIR SPOT-ON AIM. The red Mozambique spitting cobra and the black-necked spitting cobra—both of which live in Africa—spray their venom at the eyes of whatever is threatening them.

Scientists tested the aim of these two kinds of snakes by recording the interaction between the snakes and people (wearing visors) and photos of people's faces. Using a high-speed video camera, the researchers discovered the snakes "spit" with incredible accuracy: The black-necked spitting cobras hit at least one eye eight out of 10 times and the Mozambique cobras hit their target every single time.

Not only do the spitting cobras have good aim—they can launch their venom up to eight feet (2.4 m). The venom, sprayed from the snakes' fangs, is made up of toxins that cause severe pain and can even lead to blindness in the victims.

▶ Scientists used high-speed video cameras to record the accuracy of spitting cobras. Visors protected the scientists from the cloud of venom.

◀ The black-necked spitting cobra is a species of spitting cobra found mostly in sub-Saharan Africa. They can grow to a length of four to seven feet (1.2–2.1 m).

▼ The Mozambique spitting cobra has openings in the front of its fangs that allow it to shoot venom at its enemies.

EASTERN DIAMONDBACK RATTLESNAKE

DON'T SAY IT DIDN'T WARN YOU

EASTERN DIAMONDBACK RATTLESNAKES ARE THE LARGEST VENOMOUS SNAKES IN NORTH AMERICA, but they are more than willing to announce that they don't want trouble. Usually these rattlesnakes, which live in the southeastern United States, stay clear of people, **BUT IF THEY'RE STARTLED, THEY'LL SHAKE THEIR SIGNATURE RATTLE,** a noise that comes from hollow bony segments loosely attached to the ends of their tails. It produces a sound that serves as a warning: **GO AWAY!**

Baby rattlesnakes are **BORN WITHOUT A RATTLE.**

AT A GLANCE

SCIENTIFIC NAME:
Crotalus adamanteus

SIZE:
5.5 feet (1.7 m) long

HABITAT:
Shrubland, forests

☠ THE KILL

AFTER STRIKING, THE DIAMONDBACK LETS GO OF ITS PREY AND WAITS FOR IT TO DIE. Eastern diamondbacks are pit vipers, and their venom kills their victim's red blood cells and causes tissue damage. **BITES ARE VERY PAINFUL AND—UNLESS TREATED WITH AN ANTIVENOM—CAN BE FATAL FOR HUMANS.** However, this snake's most common victims are rodents and other small mammals and birds.

ONE MEAL can satisfy a rattler for two weeks.

THE BITE

AN EASTERN DIAMONDBACK DOESN'T GIVE ITS PREY ANY WARNING THAT IT'S COMING. It ambushes it—meaning it attacks by surprise. It locates the prey by scent and by sensing the heat that the animal gives off. It then strikes quickly, releasing its venom into its victim.

STILETTO SNAKE

A SNAKE WITH SWIVELED FANGS

The stiletto snake, which lives in the rainforests of southern Africa, is not only venomous, but its **FANGS ALSO DOUBLE AS A SECRET WEAPON.**

THE BITE

WHEN THE STILETTO SNAKE WANTS TO STRIKE, IT HARDLY HAS TO OPEN ITS MOUTH. Its fangs "swivel" out of the sides of its mouth, letting it stab prey without opening its jaws wide like most snakes do. Even expert snake handlers have to be extra cautious with this snake—**IT'S ALMOST IMPOSSIBLE TO HOLD ON TO WITHOUT GETTING STABBED.**

☠ THE KILL

STILETTO SNAKES' VENOM CAUSES PAIN, SWELLING, AND TISSUE DAMAGE to humans but isn't fatal. However, to the small mammals it preys on, a bite means instant death. It gets the name "stiletto" from the way its **FANGS STICK OUT OF ITS MOUTH LIKE STILETTOS—A TYPE OF DAGGER.**

AT A GLANCE

SCIENTIFIC NAME:
Atractaspis branchi

SIZE:
15 inches (40 cm)

HABITAT:
Rainforests

A stiletto snake can **JUMP** almost the length of its body.

Stiletto snakes have the **LONGEST FANGS** compared to their head size of any snake.

27

MAKING ANTIVENOM

SCIENTISTS BITE BACK AGAINST DEADLY TOXINS

ABOUT 100 YEARS AGO, A BITE FROM CERTAIN VENOMOUS SNAKES, SPIDERS, SCORPIONS, INSECTS, OR MARINE ANIMALS MEANT CERTAIN DEATH. But thanks to the development of antivenom, thousands of lives are saved every year for people who have access to it. Antivenom is a medication that boosts the body's immune system to help stop the effects of the venom. In order to make the medicine, scientists have to enlist some surprising helpers: venomous animals! Here's how it's done.

1. GETTING THE SCARY STUFF

To make antivenom, scientists first need to gather actual venom from animals. In the case of snakes, for instance, some snakes are kept in labs and monitored to make sure they are healthy. Then their venom is collected, stored in containers, and kept cold.

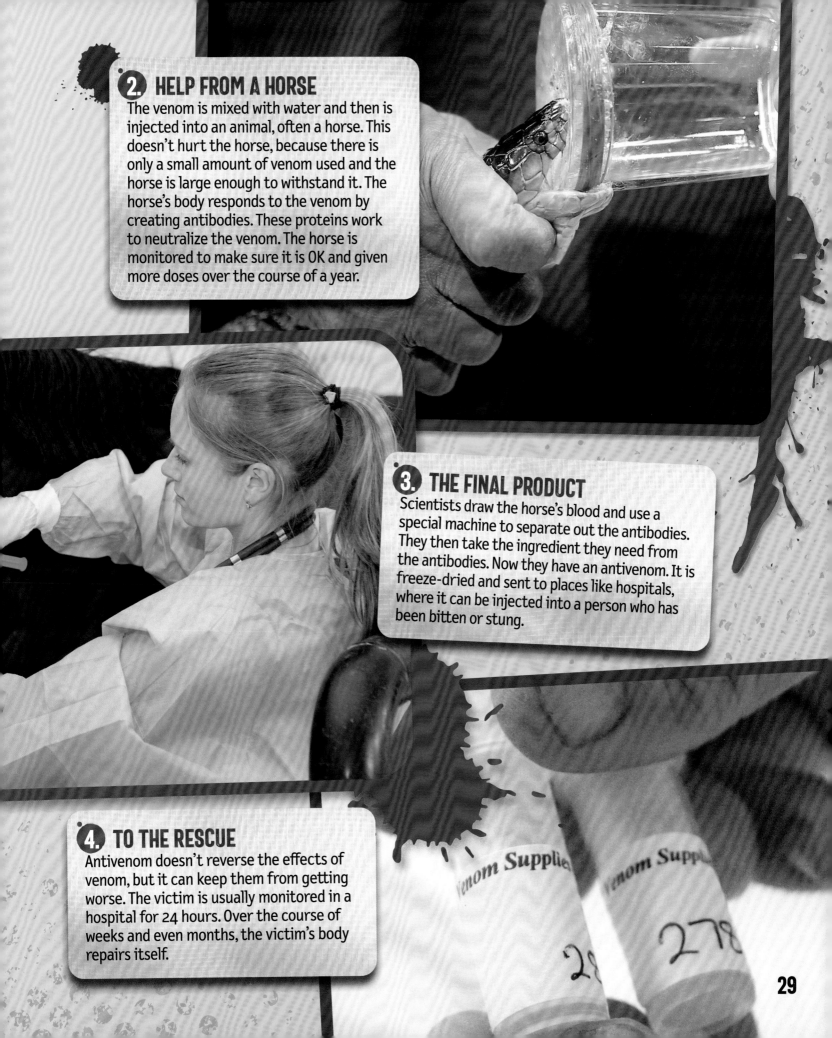

2. HELP FROM A HORSE

The venom is mixed with water and then is injected into an animal, often a horse. This doesn't hurt the horse, because there is only a small amount of venom used and the horse is large enough to withstand it. The horse's body responds to the venom by creating antibodies. These proteins work to neutralize the venom. The horse is monitored to make sure it is OK and given more doses over the course of a year.

3. THE FINAL PRODUCT

Scientists draw the horse's blood and use a special machine to separate out the antibodies. They then take the ingredient they need from the antibodies. Now they have an antivenom. It is freeze-dried and sent to places like hospitals, where it can be injected into a person who has been bitten or stung.

4. TO THE RESCUE

Antivenom doesn't reverse the effects of venom, but it can keep them from getting worse. The victim is usually monitored in a hospital for 24 hours. Over the course of weeks and even months, the victim's body repairs itself.

INLAND TAIPAN

QUIET, BUT DEADLY

Inland taipans, also known as "fierce snakes," are SOME OF THE MOST VENOMOUS SNAKES ON THE PLANET. Even though they are literally underfoot, few people ever see them. Living in remote parts of central east Australia where there is little vegetation to provide cover, the inland taipan often hangs out in deep cracks in the soil. Its skin changes color from dark brown to light green depending on the season. (The dark color helps absorb sunlight in the cold winter months, and the light color helps it stay cool in the summer.)

AT A GLANCE

SCIENTIFIC NAME:
Oxyuranus microlepidotus

SIZE:
Up to 8.2 feet (2.5 m) long

HABITAT:
Plains, wetlands

The inland taipan packs enough venom to KILL 250,000 MICE.

The inland taipan forms its body in an **S-SHAPED CURVE**, like a loaded spring ready to snap forward, **AS A WARNING DISPLAY WHEN IT'S ABOUT TO ATTACK.**

☠ THE KILL

INLAND TAIPANS TYPICALLY CORNER THEIR PREY IN A BURROW AND THEN STRIKE SEVERAL TIMES. The snake holds on to its victim while the venom quickly takes effect, stunning the prey.

⚇ THE BITE

THE INLAND TAIPAN'S FAVORITE MEAL IS A RAT, which the snake overpowers with a quick bite. **DROP FOR DROP, THEIR VENOM IS MORE TOXIC THAN ANY OTHER SNAKE'S— ONE BITE POSSESSES ENOUGH TOXIN TO KILL 100 PEOPLE.** Luckily, its natural habitat is in isolated areas of Australia, and all of its prey are small mammals.

DANGEROUS JOB: SNAKE MILKER

THE DELICATE ART OF VENOM EXTRACTION

THERE ARE JOBS THAT YOU CAN REALLY SINK YOUR TEETH INTO, AND THEN THERE ARE JOBS THAT CAN REALLY SINK THEIR TEETH INTO *YOU*! You might say both are the case with the job of a snake milker—a trained professional who gathers venom from live snakes, which is then used to make antivenom. Here's how they do it.

1. GET SELECTIVE

Snake milkers work with a group of venomous snakes that have been removed from the wild, are healthy, and are able to produce venom. The snakes aren't harmed during the milking process. They're returned to the wild after they're milked.

2. THE PICKUP

A snake is removed from its enclosure, often with the help of a long-handled hook, which isn't sharp. It is then placed on a mat, and the snake milker carefully uses the hook to keep the snake's head down so it won't attack.

3. GOT MILK?

When the snake milker is ready, they pick up the snake, with a firm grip on its head, and place its mouth on the side of a glass funnel or jar. Believe it or not, snake milkers often don't wear protective gloves. Why? They claim that holding on to the snake with their bare hands lets them feel the snake's movements better, so they can react if the snake makes a quick move. The snake milker knows just the right places to press down in order to activate the venom. The venom flows down the fangs and into the funnel. Then the snake is placed back in its enclosure to continue with its day—and its venom will go on to help a future snakebite victim.

4. READY TO GO

The venom is refrigerated or frozen and shipped to facilities that will process it into antivenom, use it in pain medications, or include it in research on other medicinal uses.

33

CHAPTER 2

SERIOUS
STINGERS

INVERTEBRATES
THAT PACK A PUNCH

SOME OF THE MOST VENOMOUS, DEADLIEST CREATURES COME IN VERY SMALL PACKAGES. Case in point: invertebrates. We're talking about animals without a backbone, like insects, worms, spiders, scorpions, and more. They're animals you might walk right by and never notice, but if you get bitten or stung by one, you won't forget it! Prepare to find out all about venomous invertebrates and their creepy-crawly world, from a spider that catches frogs to a wasp that attacks brains!

Arachnids were among the **FIRST LAND-DWELLERS,** adopting a terrestrial life at least 420 million years ago.

HONEYBEE

Honeybees can fly up to **15 MILES AN HOUR** (24 km/h) and can flap their wings nearly 200 times per second!

THE BUZZ ABOUT BEES

Black and yellow and typically keeping themselves busy hanging around flowers, honeybees are relatively unassuming. But if you look at a honeybee under a microscope, you'll discover **ITS STINGER MEANS SERIOUS BUSINESS.**

Wasps and bumblebees don't have **BARBED STINGERS** and can sting repeatedly.

THE STING

A HONEYBEE'S STINGER IS HOLLOW AND POINTED, LIKE A NEEDLE THAT DELIVERS A VACCINE. THE BEE PUMPS VENOM THROUGH THE STINGER AND INJECTS IT INTO ITS VICTIM. The outside of the stinger also has two rows of jagged blades like fishing hooks. That might sound kind of scary—and it's fair to say that getting stung by a bee does hurt!—but **HONEYBEES VERY RARELY USE THEIR SECRET WEAPON.** In fact, their stingers are only used when they (or their hives) are being threatened. Why? Because using the stinger means certain death for the bee. As the honeybee tries to pull out the stinger, it instead pulls out part of its own insides. What results is a gaping hole at the end of its abdomen.

☠ THE KILL

Honeybees use more than venom to protect themselves—**THEY ALSO PACK A POTENT CHEMICAL THAT HELPS DEFEND THEIR ENTIRE COLONY.** When a honeybee is threatened, it releases the chemical, called a pheromone, setting off a warning system to the rest of the hive. The scent of the **PHEROMONE**—which scientists describe as banana-like—**ALERTS OTHER NEARBY BEES THAT THERE IS DANGER, SIGNALING TO THEM THAT BACKUP IS NEEDED FOR AN ATTACK.**

A single honeybee produces ONE-TWELFTH OF A TEASPOON OF HONEY during its six-week life span.

AT A GLANCE

SCIENTIFIC NAME:
Apis mellifera

SIZE:
Workers: 0.4 to 0.6 inch
(1 to 1.5 cm)

HABITAT:
Found in almost all climates, from deserts to the tropics to woodlands

MORE GOOD THAN HARM

Despite their stingers, honeybees do have a sweet side. Living in colonies with one queen, all the worker bees (the ones with the stingers!) are female. Their jobs are to gather food, build honeycombs, and protect the hive. These honeybees are important pollinators for flowers, fruit, and vegetables. Transferring pollen allows plants to grow seeds and fruit. Of course, honeybees also provide honey for us to eat. A hive can produce up to 100 pounds (45 kg) of honey per year.

HOW BAD DOES A BEE STING HURT?

ONE STUDENT PUT IT TO THE TEST

WHEN IT COMES TO BEE STINGS, WHAT'S THE DIFFERENCE BETWEEN AN "OWW!" AND AN "OWWWWWW!"? One student found out (the hard way) that it all depends on where the bee decides to sting you.

When Michael Smith was a graduate student at New York's Cornell University, he became curious about which parts of the body were most sensitive to a bee sting. He decided to attach some numbers to the amount of pain suffered after being stung by a honeybee in a variety of locations. And, of course, who better to rate the honeybee stings than himself?

Smith allowed himself to be stung by a honeybee five times a day between 9 a.m. and 10 a.m. and kept careful notes. The results revealed the most painful parts on the human body that you can be stung—and the answers were a little surprising.

The worst place? The nostril! (That sting rated 9 on his pain scale of 1 to 10). Second highest on the list was the upper lip, which rated an 8.7. The armpit rated a 7, and the belly and fingertip were both 6.7. A place that's not so bad? The top of the head! It rated a mere 2.3.

▶ Michael Smith, a graduate student at Cornell University, allowed himself to be stung in 25 areas of the body to find that the nostril was the most painful. "A sting to the nostril is so painful, it's like a whole-body experience," he said.

SYDNEY FUNNEL-WEB SPIDER

WATCH YOUR STEP!

THE SYDNEY FUNNEL-WEB SPIDER IS A SNEAKY HUNTER. It sets trip-lines made of silk all around its burrow, which is usually in a cool, humid spot, like under a log or rock. It hunkers down and waits for beetles, cockroaches, or small reptiles to **STUMBLE INTO ITS TRAP.** Then it dashes out and devours them.

Funnel-web spiders **CATCH AND EAT** everything from millipedes to snails to frogs.

THE BITE

The funnel-web spider has large fangs that connect to a venom gland. **THEIR FANGS ARE STRONG ENOUGH TO PIERCE LEATHER AND HUMAN FINGERNAILS.** Because they like to hide in dark places, they sometimes slip into shoes or debris in storage sheds. Funnel-web spiders don't attack people intentionally, but if they're caught off guard by, say, a foot that has slid into the shoe they were hiding in, **THEY WILL BITE. AND THAT BITE IS TROUBLE.**

☠ THE KILL

CONSIDERED THE WORLD'S MOST VENOMOUS SPIDER, the Sydney funnel-web spider injects its victim with potent venom, immediately killing it. In humans, a bite causes rapid heart rate, increased blood pressure, difficulty breathing, and numbness around the mouth. **THE VENOM IS CAPABLE OF KILLING A PERSON IN AS LITTLE AS 15 MINUTES.** Luckily, a highly effective antivenom was developed in the 1980s, and there haven't been any deaths from this spider's bite since then.

Funnel-web spiders can **SURVIVE FOR HOURS** if they fall in water.

AT A GLANCE

SCIENTIFIC NAME:
Atrax robustus

SIZE:
0.6 to 1.4 inches
(1.5 cm to 3.5 cm)

HABITAT:
Forests, beneath houses, crevices, compost piles

SQUASHING SPIDER MYTHS

SETTING THE RECORD STRAIGHT ON SUSPICIOUS SPIDER STORIES

DON'T BELIEVE EVERYTHING YOU'VE HEARD ABOUT SPIDERS. Sure, they are creepy-crawly, but most have very little interest in bothering humans—yes, even when you're asleep! It's time to uncover the truth about spiders and put those myths to rest.

MYTH: Every year you swallow eight spiders while you sleep.

THE TRUTH: Experts say there is no evidence to back up this urban myth. Most spiders found in people's homes tend to stick to their webs, where they catch their food. Our beds (and bodies!) don't have anything to offer a spider. You can sleep well knowing that spiders are generally afraid of people, and any chance of them crawling on you at night is rare.

MYTH: Camel spiders can outrun humans.

THE TRUTH: Camel spiders, which are also called wind scorpions but are actually neither spiders nor scorpions, are about six inches (15 cm) long. They aren't venomous, but their jaws are about a third of their body length—so it's no surprise that they have a painful bite. Compared to other arachnids, they can move fast—up to 10 miles an hour (16 km/h)—but only for a very short distance. You could outrun one if you wanted to.

MYTH: Daddy longlegs have the deadliest venom.

THE TRUTH: First of all, daddy longlegs aren't spiders, although they are related to them. They don't spin webs like spiders, and they don't have venomous sacs. Some do secrete a poison (a harmful chemical that is not injected into prey) that could affect small predators, but not humans.

BLACK WIDOW SPIDER

LADY OF THE HOUR

FEMALE BLACK WIDOW SPIDERS ARE RECOGNIZED BY THE RED HOURGLASS MARKINGS ON THEIR ABDOMENS and are notorious for their bite. This is for good reason: They are the most venomous spiders in North America, **PACKING VENOM 15 TIMES STRONGER THAN A RATTLESNAKE'S.** Male black widows get less attention for a few reasons—they are about half the size of the females, produce far less venom, and are harmless to humans.

Black widow spiders' legs are covered in an **OILY SUBSTANCE** that keeps them from sticking to their webs.

THE BITE

BLACK WIDOWS PRIMARILY USE THEIR FANGS WHEN THEY EAT, biting insects they've caught in their webs to inject digestive enzymes that liquefy the prey's body, which they then suck up.

☠ THE KILL

INSECTS AREN'T A FEMALE BLACK WIDOW'S ONLY PREY—MALE BLACK WIDOWS ARE, TOO. After mating, the female sometimes bites and kills her partner. When people are bit by a black widow, it can cause **MUSCLE ACHES, NAUSEA, AND DIFFICULTY BREATHING,** but fatalities are relatively rare.

AT A GLANCE

SCIENTIFIC NAME:
Latrodectus

SIZE:
1.5 inches (3.8 cm)

HABITAT:
Forests, beneath houses, crevices, compost piles

Black widow spiders live in **EVERY U.S. STATE** except Alaska.

FACT
OR FICTION?
HERE'S THE SCOOP!

DO YOU KNOW WHICH OF THESE RUMORS ARE REAL AND WHICH ARE BALONEY? Read on for the real story!

FACT OR FICTION?

Dracula ants bite people and drink their blood.

FICTION—but they do bite their own children! Dracula ants get their name for the way the queen and worker ants sometimes feed off the blood of their young. It may seem creepy, but the good news is this unique eating habit doesn't end in death for the young. By the time they reach adulthood, young ants are often left with some bite-mark scars, but other than that, they are unharmed by their relatives' nibbles.

FACT OR FICTION?

Scorpions glow in the dark.

FACT! Scorpions have a substance in their exoskeletons that makes them glow blue-green under ultraviolet light. Scientists aren't sure why they glow, but they have a few theories. The glow may help scorpions distract prey while they are preparing to attack, or it may help them find other scorpions. It may even help protect them against parasites.

FACT OR FICTION?

The color of your clothes can attract mosquitoes.

FACT! Mosquitoes are more attracted to dark clothing than light-colored clothing. Mosquitoes use sight—and also rely on an ability to detect smell and heat—to find blood; because they see dark objects better than light ones, they are more apt to head toward people wearing dark colors.

FACT OR FICTION?

Tarantulas fling their eyeballs at attackers.

FICTION—but not too far from the truth! When some species of tarantulas are attacked, they fling barbed hairs from their bellies to distract the predator. When the flinging is done, the tarantula will often be left with a bald spot!

DEATHSTALKER SCORPION

LIVING UP TO ITS NAME

Built for an attack, scorpions strike from the back. Of the nearly 2,000 species of scorpions, only a few dozen pack a venomous punch **CAPABLE OF KILLING A PERSON.** And as you might guess by its name, **THE DEATHSTALKER SCORPION IS ONE OF THEM.**

Scorpions have two eyes on top of their heads and up to **FIVE PAIRS OF EYES** in front.

THE STING

Found in the deserts of North Africa and the Middle East, the deathstalker scorpion has **TINY ORGANS IN ITS LEGS THAT CAN DETECT VIBRATIONS IN THE SAND.** These sensations tell it the direction and distance of prey, which includes spiders, centipedes, and other scorpions. When it finds its dinner, the deathstalker attacks by delivering its powerful venom through its tail. **THE LAST SEGMENT OF ITS TAIL, CALLED THE TELSON, CONTAINS VENOM SACS AND A BARB THAT DELIVERS TOXINS.**

☠ THE KILL

THE DEATHSTALKER MAY BE ONE OF THE MOST VENOMOUS SCORPIONS IN THE WORLD, BUT ITS PINCERS ARE RELATIVELY WEAK. It relies on its venom to work quickly, which paralyzes prey, keeping it from moving. Then it has time to settle in and **DEVOUR ITS DINNER.**

When food is scarce, scorpions can live on just **ONE INSECT PER YEAR.**

AT A GLANCE

SCIENTIFIC NAME:
Leiurus quinquestriatus

SIZE:
Three to four inches
(8 to 10 cm)

HABITAT:
Dry desert landscapes

VENOM
AND THE HUMAN BODY
FROM ANNOYING ITCH TO SUPER SERIOUS

WHAT HAPPENS WHEN YOU GET BITTEN BY A SNAKE OR SPIDER? Or get stung by a bee or jellyfish? Well, for starters, it hurts—sometimes a little, sometimes a lot! What happens next depends on the type of venom that has entered your body, how much venom was released, and how your body reacts to the toxins.

Not all venom is the same. Some may cause bleeding, and others may cause paralysis—shutting off your body's nervous system. Depending on the size of the person, the amount and type of venom released, and how far away medical help is, the effects can range from an annoying itch to death. Here's a rundown on the range of the human body's reactions to a venomous bite or sting—from mild to extreme.

😠 **MILD** The moment you spot a mosquito landing on your arm, you know what's going to happen next: There's going to be some swelling, some redness, and a whole lot of itching. When a mosquito breaks your skin with its mouth and injects its saliva into you, your body's immune system kicks in and produces histamine to help reject this foreign substance. You'll experience increased blood flow, which helps white blood cells rush to the area—causing the swelling. The itching sensation is a response by your nerve cells to the histamine. The good news? After a few days, your body calms down, the swelling goes away, and the itch will be a thing of the past.

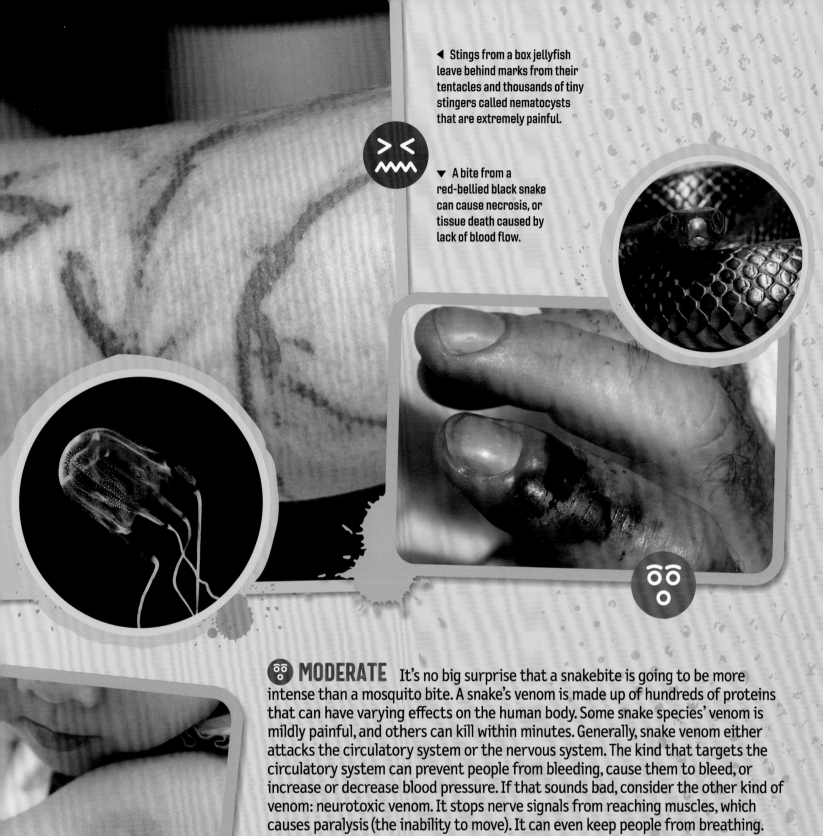

◀ Stings from a box jellyfish leave behind marks from their tentacles and thousands of tiny stingers called nematocysts that are extremely painful.

▼ A bite from a red-bellied black snake can cause necrosis, or tissue death caused by lack of blood flow.

MODERATE It's no big surprise that a snakebite is going to be more intense than a mosquito bite. A snake's venom is made up of hundreds of proteins that can have varying effects on the human body. Some snake species' venom is mildly painful, and others can kill within minutes. Generally, snake venom either attacks the circulatory system or the nervous system. The kind that targets the circulatory system can prevent people from bleeding, cause them to bleed, or increase or decrease blood pressure. If that sounds bad, consider the other kind of venom: neurotoxic venom. It stops nerve signals from reaching muscles, which causes paralysis (the inability to move). It can even keep people from breathing. Luckily, antivenoms have been developed for many of the most toxic snake venoms.

EXTREME There are thousands of species of jellyfish and only a few dozen whose stings are painful. But there is one species, the box jellyfish, that is in a category of its own. Box jellyfish, which sting with their tentacles, can leave behind thousands of tiny stingers called nematocysts in your skin. The stingers release venom, causing intense pain. Box jellyfish stings attack the nervous system and can cause an increase in heart rate or blood pressure and paralysis—even death.

MOSQUITO

A SMALL INSECT WITH A BIG BITE

The deadliest venomous creature in the world isn't a snake. It isn't a spider. It isn't an exotic-looking spiky fish. **IT'S AN INSECT THAT'S LESS THAN AN INCH (2.5 CM) LONG, AND ITS BITE DOESN'T EVEN HURT ALL THAT MUCH.** It's the mosquito. There are more than 3,000 species of mosquitoes—most of which are harmless, beyond creating an annoying itch. But three particular species—found mainly in tropical regions—are **PRIMARILY TO BLAME FOR THE SPREAD OF HUMAN DISEASES THAT KILL MORE THAN A MILLION PEOPLE WORLDWIDE EVERY YEAR.**

MALE MOSQUITOES eat nectar and are **POLLINATORS,** just like bees.

THE BITE

Mosquitoes aren't trying to be vicious. **FEMALE MOSQUITOES TAKE BLOOD FROM WARM-BLOODED ANIMALS, INCLUDING HUMANS, AS A SOURCE OF PROTEIN FOR THEIR EGGS.** While she eats, a female mosquito uses her proboscis—which has two long, hollow tubes, like syringes—to inject venomous saliva into her victim. Humans react to a mosquito bite by producing histamine, which is what causes the **RED WELT ON YOUR SKIN AND ITCHINESS THAT CAN LAST A FEW DAYS.**

A FEW SPECIES OF MOSQUITOES CARRY INFECTIOUS DISEASES AND PARASITES THAT ENTER THEIR HOSTS. Those diseases include malaria, yellow fever, dengue fever, and West Nile virus. Keep in mind, the vast majority of mosquitoes do little more than cause you to itch. **THERE ARE WAYS TO PREVENT MOSQUITO BITES,** such as using insect repellent and bug nets, wearing clothing that covers your body, and avoiding areas with standing water. Vaccines offer protection against some of the harmful diseases that mosquitoes carry.

AT A GLANCE

SCIENTIFIC NAME:
Culicidae (family)

SIZE:
.125 to .75 inch (3 to 20 mm)

HABITAT:
Moist soil, standing water

Mosquitoes are more active during a **FULL MOON.**

MMM, WHAT TASTY BLOOD YOU HAVE

Have you ever gone on a hike or camping trip and come back covered in mosquito bites, while your friends came back itch-free? It's not just bad luck. Some people are more likely to be bit by mosquitoes than others.

It's in your blood. Human blood is classified into four main blood groups—A, B, AB, and O. A study found that mosquitoes land on people with type O blood twice as often as people with type A blood.

Attracted to athletes. When you exercise, your body produces heat and lactic acid—two things mosquitoes are drawn to. Better run fast, because exercising makes you more susceptible to catching a mosquito's interest.

Sweet smelly feet. Your feet are hosts to bacteria—the reason they have a tendency to get a little stinky. It turns out mosquitoes are drawn to that scent, which is why mosquito bites around the feet and ankles are so common.

THE ODD SQUAD

WATCH OUT FOR THESE WILDLY WEIRD CREATURES

SOMETIMES STANDING OUT CAN GET YOU JUST WHAT YOU NEED.
These critters don't get by on only their unusual looks—they'll surprise you with their fatal bites, powerful headbutts, or a sneaky stinky smell!

A FROG WITH A VENOMOUS HEADBUTT

The Greening's frog really knows how to use its head. The frog delivers toxic mucus that covers its body by using the spines on top of its head. The mucus is more venomous than the bite of some pit viper snakes. When threatened, the frog headbutts predators, poking them with its spiky head and releasing the mucus into the wound. The frog's defense mechanism comes in handy in its forest home in Brazil. During dry seasons, it will burrow in a hole and plug the entrance with its head. This helps keep its body moist, and its camouflaged head acts as protection. If a predator comes sniffing around, it will get a toxic poke.

ZOMBIE WASP

With a nickname like "zombie wasp," you know this insect must be weird. The jewel wasp uses its stinger to inject venom into cockroaches' brains! The venom paralyzes the cockroach, and the wasp lays eggs on its legs. When the eggs hatch, the larvae chew a hole in the cockroach's abdomen and feed on it.

DEEP-SEA VENOM

The first venomous crustacean discovered is blind, only a few inches long, and lives in deep underwater caves. And it turns its prey into milkshakes with its bite. *Speleonectes tulumensis*, which lives in Mexico and Central America, uses its fangs to inject venom into shrimp and small fish, liquefying them so they can be slurped up.

ANT WANNABE

If you can't beat 'em, join 'em. That's how the West African savanna frog gets along with the venomous, stinging stink ants it lives near. Normally, when the ants are disturbed, they attack, stinging and releasing dangerous venom. But the savanna frog lives among them in their moist underground nests during the dry season. How? The frog releases a chemical that tricks the ants into believing it is one of their own, so they leave it be.

BULLET ANT

A STING THAT STICKS AROUND

THEY DON'T CALL IT THE WORLD'S MOST PAINFUL INSECT FOR NOTHING. The bullet ant's sting is fierce. Living at the base of trees in Central and South American rainforests in colonies of up to 2,500 individuals, bullet ants are one of the largest ants on Earth—about as long as a small paper clip. When they get mad, watch out: **THEIR STING STAYS WITH YOU.**

A sting from a bullet ant doesn't cause much **SWELLING**—or even leave a mark.

THE STING

WHEN DISTURBED, BULLET ANTS BECOME AGGRESSIVE AND WILL STING to defend themselves. For example, they will sting when their nest is attacked by predators such as frogs.

☠ THE KILL

Bullet ants are more interested in gathering nectar than stinging, but when they do sting, **THEY RELEASE A NEUROTOXIC VENOM THAT KEEPS ATTACKERS FROM BEING ABLE TO MOVE.** Occasionally the ants will have run-ins with people; the sting can cause extreme pain that can last for several days.

A bullet ant sting is said to be 30 times **MORE PAINFUL** than a bee sting.

AT A GLANCE

SCIENTIFIC NAME:
Paraponera clavata

SIZE:
One inch (2.5 cm)

HABITAT:
Rainforest

EXTREME ATTACKERS

VENOMOUS BITES AND STINGS ARE JUST THE BEGINNING FOR THESE NEXT-LEVEL INVERTEBRATES

FOR SOME CRITTERS, HAVING ONE TRICK UP THEIR SLEEVE JUST ISN'T ENOUGH TO GET THE JOB DONE. These invertebrates take their attacks to the next level—by being oversized, extra disguised, or possessing ninja-style killing tactics.

GOLIATH BIRD–EATING TARANTULA

Where do you begin with the Goliath bird-eating tarantula? Maybe its size: This spider's body is up to 4.75 inches (12 cm) long and its leg span is as wide as a basketball, making it the biggest tarantula in the world. But then there are its fangs, which are an inch (2.5 cm) long. Its venom is powerful enough to subdue prey such as mice and frogs. (Despite its name, these tarantulas rarely eat birds!) When threatened, it lets out a unique warning by rubbing its hairs together, creating a sound that can be heard 15 feet (4.6 m) away.

ASSASSIN FLY

You can tell this insect means business just by its name. Assassin flies have venomous saliva, which they use to feast on spiders and insects such as bees, wasps, dragonflies, and other flies. Found throughout the world, the assassin fly has a vicious mode of attack: It perches itself on a rock, plant, or tree branch, then when it sees prey, it flies after its victim, grabs it, and injects it with saliva. The saliva serves two purposes: It kills the prey almost instantly, and it liquefies its body—which the assassin fly slurps up.

SOUTHERN FLANNEL MOTH

Can a creature with the word "flannel" in its name really be all that frightening? Why yes, it can. The caterpillar of the southern flannel moth is among the most venomous creatures in North America. While it appears soft and fuzzy, its spines are connected to venomous gland cells that can poke through your skin. Better not pick one up: Handling the caterpillar can cause intense pain lasting 12 or more hours.

ASIAN GIANT HORNET

The biggest wasp on the planet is also one of the most venomous insects. At up to two inches (5 cm) long with a quarter-inch (6-mm)-long stinger, the Asian giant hornet delivers a toxin that is capable of killing a person. But its main prey is the honeybee. Found across East and Southeast Asia, one Asian giant hornet can kill 300 honeybees in an hour. A swarm of hornets can take out an entire colony.

STUNNING SEA CREATURES

VENOM UNDERWATER

IF ALL THE VENOMOUS CREATURES ON LAND ARE MAKING YOU THINK ABOUT RUNNING FOR THE SEA, YOU MIGHT WANT TO THINK AGAIN. Some of the deadliest animals on Earth lurk in the ocean. From fish to jellies to octopuses to sea anemones, venomous sea life comes in all shapes and sizes—with varying levels of potency. When marine animals strike people, it's almost always in self-defense after they are threatened or taken by surprise. But when venomous marine life *want* to strike, look out! They quite literally stun their prey when they attack. Take a deep breath and head undersea to find out about these super stingers!

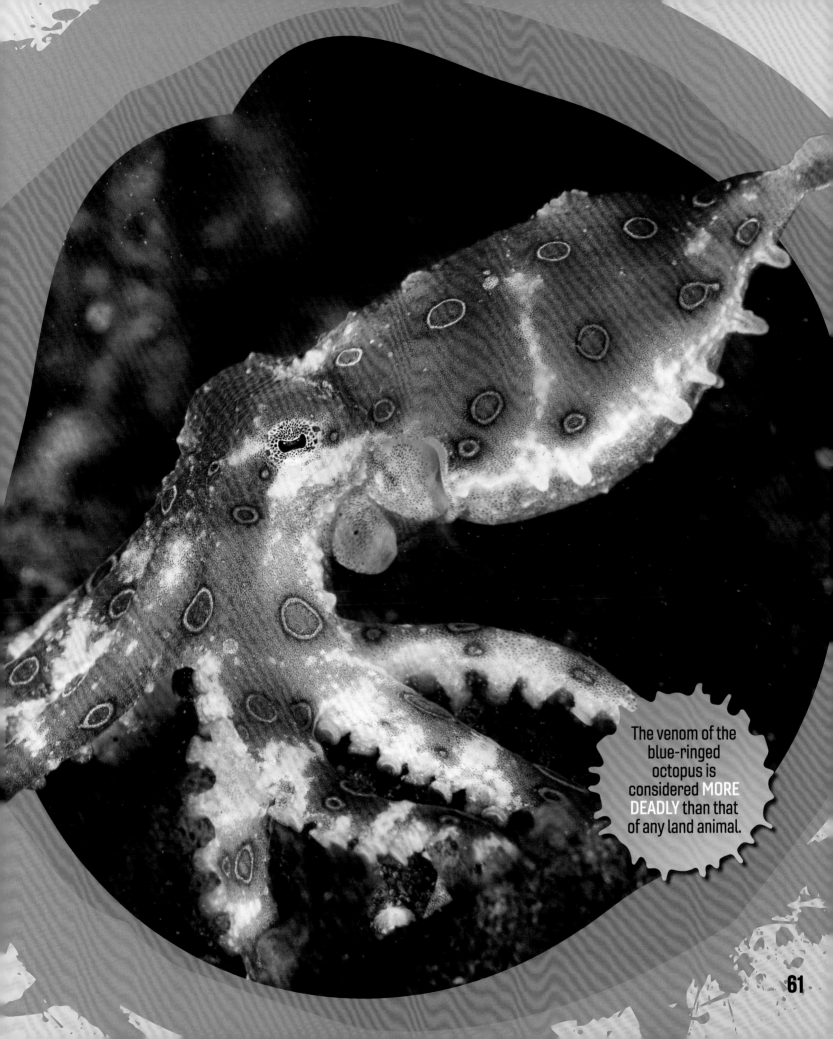

The venom of the blue-ringed octopus is considered **MORE DEADLY** than that of any land animal.

BOX JELLYFISH

STING OPERATION

It's hard to imagine that a creature so mesmerizing could **UNLEASH SOME OF THE MOST HARMFUL VENOM ON THE PLANET.** A box jellyfish's toxins are so intense that they attack the heart, nervous system, *and* skin cells of its prey, instantly stunning or killing them. Box jellyfish, which live in the waters off of northern Australia and throughout the Indo-Pacific, get their name from the boxy shape of their body. While most jellyfish are "drifters"—meaning they drift along wherever the oceans' currents take them—**BOX JELLYFISH SWIM AT SPEEDS OF UP TO 4.5 MILES AN HOUR (7 KM/H).**

Box jellyfish have **24 EYES.**

THE STING

Why so venomous? Box jellyfish need to **TAKE OUT THEIR PREY—MOSTLY SHRIMP AND FISH—QUICKLY** so they don't damage their delicate tentacles, which can stretch 10 feet (30 m) long. Those tentacles—and there are up to 15 of them—are covered in some **5,000 STINGING CELLS.**

☠ THE KILL

THE JELLYFISH'S STING IMMEDIATELY KILLS SMALL PREY. THEN THE JELLY SWALLOWS ITS LUNCH THROUGH AN OPENING INSIDE ITS BOX-SHAPED BODY. When humans have run-ins with box jellyfish, they can endure pain for weeks. They can even have scars where the tentacles stung. Under rare circumstances, people have died from heart failure after an encounter.

One of a box jellyfish's eyes is ALWAYS LOOKING UP toward the water's surface.

AT A GLACE

SCIENTIFIC NAME:
Cubozoa (class)

SIZE:
10 feet (30 m) long;
10 inches (25 cm) across

HABITAT:
Coastal waters

WILLING TO TAKE A STING

Sea turtles eat box jellies for lunch! The highly venomous box jellyfish is just a gooey, delicious snack for a sea turtle! Sea turtles aren't fazed by the jellyfish's sting. Why? The turtles' protective shells cover much of their bodies, and they tend to only eat the top, nonstinging part of the jellyfish, avoiding the venomous tentacles.

VENOM FROM DOWN UNDER

WHICH OF AUSTRALIA'S ANIMALS ARE THE MOST DANGEROUS?

AUSTRALIA IS FAMOUS FOR BEING A HOTBED OF DANGEROUS ANIMALS. But how do you measure which is the *most* dangerous? Scientists recently studied data from 42,000 Australian hospital admissions from venomous stings and bites to find some answers. It turns out that even though marine animals are some of the world's most venomous creatures, they aren't the most dangerous to humans. Snakes and spiders aren't either. Surprisingly, small venomous creatures are all the buzz.

NUMBER OF HOSPITALIZATIONS from a venomous sting or bite over a 12-year period in Australia:

Bees, hornets, and wasps	12,351
Spiders	11,994
Snakes	6,123
Ticks and ants	4,533
Marine animals	3,707
Other unspecified animal or plant	536
Other specified animal	151
Centipedes and millipedes	119
Scorpions	61
Other specified plant	44

◀ The sting of the marble scorpion can cause severe pain and a burning sensation for several hours.

◄ The stings from bees, hornets, and wasps and bites from snakes, such as this wild eastern brown snake, caused an equal number of deaths over a 12-year period in Australia.

▲ The stinging jack jumper ant is named for the way it walks— like it's hopping. It grasps its victims in its jaws, then bends and stings them.

◄ There are more than 40 species of funnel-web spiders in Australia. Not all of them are deadly, but they all have sharp, powerful fangs that can penetrate shoe leather. The deadliest is the Sydney funnel-web spider. A single bite can kill a human in 15 minutes.

NUMBER OF DEATHS from a venomous bite or sting over a 12-year period in Australia:

Bees, hornets, and wasps	27
Snakes	27
Ticks and ants	5
Marine animals (box jellyfish)	3
Unknown	2
Spiders	0
Centipedes and millipedes	0
Scorpions	0
Other specified animal	0
Other specified plant	0
Other unspecified animal or plant	0

STINGRAY

Some stingrays move through the water by **FLAPPING THEIR FINS LIKE A BIRD.**

THE PAIN IS IN THE NAME

STINGRAYS LIVE UP TO THEIR NAME. Swimming with their fluttery fins in temperate and tropical waters around the world, stingrays drag a dangerous tail behind them. **WHEN SWISHED LIKE A WHIP, IT SENDS ATTACKERS ON THEIR WAY.**

THE STING

Stingrays, which are related to sharks, **OFTEN LIE PARTLY BURIED IN THE SAND, EATING WORMS AND MOLLUSKS.** There's no need to use their stingers on these slow-moving prey. **BUT IF THEY FIND THEMSELVES UNDER THE FOOT OF A SNORKELER, OR ATTACKED BY ANOTHER FISH, THEY LASH OUT.**

☠ THE KILL

Most stingrays have sharp SERRATED OR NOTCHED SPINES IN THEIR TAILS THAT DELIVER VENOM POTENT ENOUGH TO FEND OFF SHARKS, one of the stingrays' top predators. In humans, a sting is painful but rarely deadly.

A short-tailed stingray weighs more than a SIBERIAN TIGER.

AT A GLANCE

SCIENTIFIC NAME:
Myliobatoidei (suborder)

SIZE:
Up to 6.5 feet (2 m)

HABITAT:
Temperate and tropical oceans

ANCIENT GREEK STINGRAYS

Some stories of the stingray's deadly tail are thousands of years old. Odysseus, the hero of a 2,700-year-old poem called the *Odyssey,* is said to have been killed by a spear tipped with the spine of a stingray. He died from the wound. But in ancient Greece, stingray venom wasn't just a thing of fables—it was used in a very practical way. Dentists at the time used the venom to numb their patients!

67

GEOGRAPHY CONE SNAIL

SLOW BUT DEADLY

THE UNASSUMING GEOGRAPHY CONE SNAIL IS A MERE SIX INCHES (15 CM) LONG, has an intricately patterned shell, and spends the daytime hours buried under sand. WHO WOULD EVER SUSPECT IT IS ONE OF THE DEADLIEST CREATURES ON EARTH?

THE STING

There are plenty of super-venomous creatures in the sea, but it's HOW THE GEOGRAPHY CONE SNAIL DELIVERS ITS VENOM THAT MAKES IT UNIQUE. Being a snail, it gets around pretty slowly. When it attacks its prey—like worms and fish—it needs to kill fast, or the prey would simply swim or wiggle away. Here's how it does it: The cone snail catches the attention of its prey by waving a long appendage, called a proboscis, like a lure. Then it brings out its weapon. Cone snails have a modified tooth called a radula. It's SHARP, LIKE A HARPOON, AND HOLLOW, LIKE A MEDICAL NEEDLE. The cone snail launches this tooth at its distracted prey, and before the prey knows what's happening, the snail has delivered its toxic venom.

A cone snail's **TOOTH IS SHARP** enough to pierce a diver's wet suit.

☠ THE KILL

Of the 500 species of cone snails, **THE GEOGRAPHY CONE, WHICH LIVES IN THE REEFS OF THE INDO-PACIFIC, IS THE MOST LETHAL.** Its venom is a mix of hundreds of different toxins that attack the nerve cells, paralyzing prey. Then the snail can start eating. There is no antivenom for humans. The only medical treatment is simply to keep the person alive until the toxins run their course. The amount of **VENOM A GEOGRAPHY CONE SNAIL CARRIES HAS THE POTENTIAL TO KILL 15 PEOPLE.** Luckily, fatalities are low—only a few dozen people are known to have died from their sting.

AT A GLANCE
SCIENTIFIC NAME:
Conus geographus

SIZE:
Four to six inches (10 to 15 cm)

HABITAT:
Ocean reefs

If a cone snail damages its **HARPOON TOOTH** in an attack, it can grow another one.

FROM DANGEROUS
TO LIFESAVING
VENOMOUS ANIMALS TO THE RESCUE!

SOME VENOMOUS ANIMALS CAN BOTH THREATEN AND SAVE PEOPLE'S LIVES. Scientists have discovered that the venoms from some of the most dangerous creatures have properties that can actually improve symptoms of certain medical conditions. By studying venom, researchers have created medicines to treat conditions like diabetes, high blood pressure, pain, and more. Here are four heroic venomous creatures.

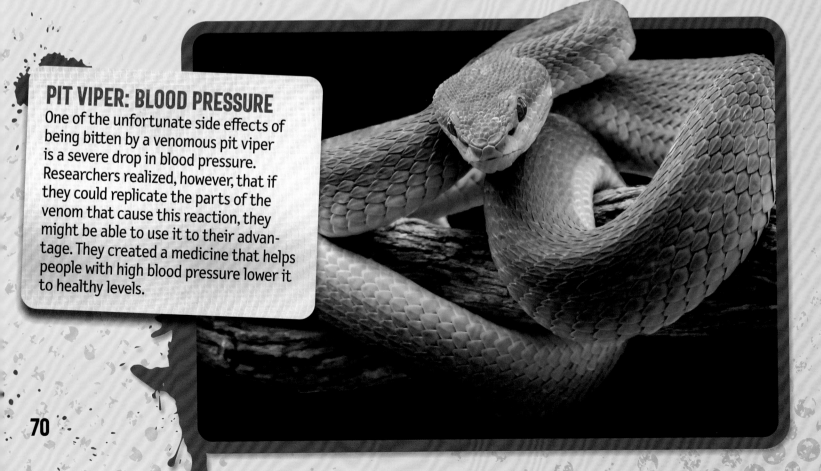

PIT VIPER: BLOOD PRESSURE

One of the unfortunate side effects of being bitten by a venomous pit viper is a severe drop in blood pressure. Researchers realized, however, that if they could replicate the parts of the venom that cause this reaction, they might be able to use it to their advantage. They created a medicine that helps people with high blood pressure lower it to healthy levels.

TARANTULA: PAINKILLER

A bite from a tarantula is painful, but the venom of the Peruvian green velvet tarantula is actually a good pain *reliever*. Researchers figured out that the special makeup of the venom prevents messages of pain from being delivered to the brain. That means when something really hurts, your brain doesn't necessarily get the message. Researchers hope to further develop medicine made from the venom to make a more effective pain reliever.

CONE SNAIL: CHRONIC PAIN

Talk about dual personalities: A cone snail's venom can either bring death or relief from serious pain, depending on how it's used. While the cone snail typically uses its venom to paralyze prey, researchers discovered something in its venom that provides long-lasting pain relief for people who haven't had luck with traditional pain relief medicine.

GILA MONSTER: TYPE 2 DIABETES

The venomous saliva of the Gila monster, that slow-moving lizard of the U.S. Southwest and northwestern Mexico, is helping diabetic patients. People with Type 2 diabetes either don't produce enough insulin—a hormone that controls sugar in your cells—or their body resists the effects of insulin. Researchers figured out that the makeup of the Gila monster's saliva helps kick the body's insulin production into gear. A medicine was developed from this observation, and now Gila monster spit is saving lives!

71

BLUE-RINGED OCTOPUS

OBSERVE THE WARNING SIGNS

AN OCTOPUS THE SIZE OF A GOLF BALL? SOUNDS ADORABLE, RIGHT? TRY DEADLY. Living in sandy shallow coral reefs and tide pools in waters from northern Australia to Japan, the blue-ringed octopus hides out in rock crevices and empty seashells. When it emerges, **IT'S PREPARED TO UNLEASH A VENOMOUS BITE**—and if it happens to get caught off guard, it puts on a show.

Unlike most other octopuses, the blue-ringed octopus DOESN'T PRODUCE INK.

THE BITE

When snagging lunch—like crabs, shrimp, or fish—the octopus isn't afraid to take a big bite. This is how it injects its venom, which is **CONSIDERED MORE TOXIC THAN THE VENOM OF ANY LAND ANIMAL.** The venom paralyzes the prey, and the octopus uses its parrot-like beak to dig in and feast.

Even though it **CAN BE DEADLY**, a blue-ringed octopus's bite isn't painful.

☠ THE KILL

The blue-ringed octopus doesn't only kill small prey, **IT CARRIES ENOUGH VENOM TO KILL 26 HUMANS AT ONE TIME.** In humans, the venom blocks nerve signals and causes parts of the body to become immobile. Other symptoms are loss of sight, nausea, and difficulty breathing. There isn't an antivenom to counter the effects, so it's best for prey of all sizes to observe the octopus's warning sign: **WHEN IT FEELS THREATENED, THE OCTOPUS'S IRIDESCENT BLUE RINGS APPEAR TO GLOW.** That's the cue to swim away—fast.

AT A GLANCE

SCIENTIFIC NAME:
Hapalochlaena maculosa

SIZE:
Eight inches (20 cm),
including its arms

HABITAT:
Ocean reefs

POISONOUS *OR* VENOMOUS

DO YOU KNOW THE DIFFERENCE?

SOME ANIMALS ARE POISONOUS AND SOME ARE VENOMOUS. To figure out which category an animal falls into, you have to know some specifics about their superpowers. *Poisonous* animals transfer their toxins when they're touched or eaten. *Venomous* animals inject their toxins, usually through a stinger or fangs. Either way, these creatures know how to get the job done!

DART FROG

Poison dart frogs' brilliant colors are beautiful to the eye, but they also serve as a warning to predators: Back off! Poison dart frogs are some of the most poisonous animals on Earth. A toxic slime on their skin can be deadly to predators that touch them. That's something the indigenous Emberá people of Colombia have used to their advantage for hundreds of years. Emberá hunters use dart frog toxin on the tips of their blowgun darts, which immediately take down the birds and other small animals they hunt.

POISONOUS

VENOMOUS

LIONFISH

Spiky spines are the perfect tools for lionfish to deliver their venom. When a lionfish pokes its victim, glands underneath the spine release venom that travels through two grooves in the spine and into the victim.

PUFFERFISH

When a predator tries to snag a pufferfish, it gets a mouthful ... of toxins that are lethal to marine life and potentially deadly to humans. The pufferfish doesn't make the poison in its body—it eats other small animals that eat toxin-producing bacteria that the pufferfish stores in its body.

POISONOUS

VENOMOUS

SCORPIONFISH

Like their on-land namesakes, scorpionfish pack a venomous punch. Bottom-dwelling fish that are experts at blending in, scorpionfish have spines containing potent venom that is dangerous to humans and deadly to both predators and prey.

STONEFISH

WATCH YOUR STEP

The name "stonefish" perfectly describes this venomous fish: ITS BUMPY SKIN BLENDS IN SO WELL WITH ROCKS ON THE OCEAN FLOOR THAT IT IS ALMOST IMPOSSIBLE TO SPOT. But if you do step on one, you're in for more than just a stubbed toe.

THE STING

Found in the shallow coastal waters of northern Australia, STONEFISH SPEND THEIR DAYS MOTIONLESS, PARTIALLY BURIED AMONG REEF, CORAL, AND AQUATIC PLANTS. They "play rock," patiently waiting until their prey—mainly small fish—swim by. Then, in the flash of an eye, the stonefish opens its mouth, creating a vacuum, and it sucks up its prey.

A stonefish's venomous side has nothing to do with catching food. It is all about self-defense against its predatory foes, like sharks and rays. STONEFISH HAVE 13 SHARP SPINES ON THEIR DORSAL FINS, EACH WITH TWO GLANDS CONTAINING VENOM that can be released at a moment's notice.

AT A GLANCE

SCIENTIFIC NAME:
Synanceia

SIZE:
Up to 18.5 inches (47 cm)

HABITAT:
Coral or rocky reefs, mudflats, and estuaries

Stonefish are the **WORLD'S MOST VENOMOUS** fish.

☠ THE KILL

There are no friendly pokes when it comes to stonefish. SWIMMERS WHO SOMETIMES ACCIDENTALLY STEP ON A STONEFISH SHOULD HEAD STRAIGHT TO THE HOSPITAL. Symptoms include intense pain, swelling, a drop in blood pressure, paralysis, and difficulty breathing. LUCKILY, AN ANTIVENOM HAS BEEN DEVELOPED THAT NEUTRALIZES THE TOXIN IF TAKEN WITHIN A FEW HOURS.

Some stonefish are CAMOUFLAGED ON THE SEAFLOOR by the algae that grow on them.

SEA ANEMONE

CLINGY AND STINGING

SEA ANEMONES COULD BE MISTAKEN FOR A FLASHY EXOTIC SEA PLANT, BUT THEY'RE ACTUALLY MARINE ANIMALS WILLING TO STING FOR FOOD. Sea anemones spend the majority of their lives attached to rocks on the seafloor or on coral reefs, waiting patiently for fish to pass—and, if the anemones are lucky, get caught in their venomous tentacles. MORE THAN A THOUSAND SPECIES OF SEA ANEMONES LIVE IN OCEANS AROUND THE WORLD, and they range in size from half an inch (1.3 cm) to six feet (1.8 m).

THE STING

THEY MAY NOT LOOK THE PART, BUT SEA ANEMONES ARE MEAT-EATING ANIMALS. If a fish happens to brush by, they will inject it with a toxin that causes immediate paralysis.

Some species of sea anemone can live for more than **50 YEARS.**

Once they've stunned their prey and it can't swim away, **THE ANEMONE USES ITS TENTACLES TO PULL THE FISH INSIDE ITS MOUTH.**

If a predator threatens them, sea anemones can **DETACH FROM THEIR ROCK OR REEF,** slowly slide on their bases, and reattach someplace else.

AT A GLANCE

SCIENTIFIC NAME:
Actiniaria (order)

SIZE:
0.5 inch (1.3 cm)
to six feet (1.8 m)

HABITAT:
Tidal zones to depths of
33,000 feet (10,000 m)
in all oceans

A FRIENDLY ALLIANCE

A fish that makes its home inside a sea anemone's tentacles? With a name like "clownfish," you'd think it was just acting silly. Believe it or not, it's a win-win living situation for both the clownfish and the sea anemone.

Clownfish have a protective layer of mucus around their bodies that makes them immune to sea anemones' venomous sting. It's safe for them to live within the tentacles, where they can avoid other predators. The sea anemone also wins in this partnership: Clownfish chase away butterflyfish, which like to eat anemones. Even though sea anemones are animals, they—like plants—need fertilizer to grow their tentacles. Clownfish to the rescue! They fertilize the anemones with their waste.

SPURDOG

ALL STING AND NO BARK

These sharks wield more than just sharp teeth. Spurdogs—also known as spiny dogfish or skittle dogs—would feel like a fish out of water on a leash or at a dog park. The "dog" in the second half of their name comes from their hunting technique. Spurdogs sometimes GROUP TOGETHER IN THE HUNDREDS TO SEEK OUT PREY like herring, mackerel, and even jellyfish. They often work together— like a pack of dogs—to chase after their prey, chomping down on them with sharp teeth.

THE STING

These members of the dogfish family get the "spur" in their name from the VENOMOUS SPINES IN FRONT OF EACH OF THEIR DORSAL FINS. When attacking predators—like orcas, other large sharks, and seals—get too close, spurdogs arch their backs and poke the predator with their spines, which RELEASE A VENOMOUS TOXIN.

Female spurdogs have one of the LONGEST PREGNANCIES of any vertebrate—up to two years!

Newborn spurdogs **HUNT FISH TWO TO THREE TIMES** their size.

☠ THE KILL.

While the spurdogs' **SHARP TEETH ARE DEADLY,** their venom is just toxic enough to fend off attacking predators and only causes **SWELLING AND DISCOMFORT IN HUMANS.**

AT A GLANCE

SCIENTIFIC NAME:
Squalus acanthias

SIZE:
Up to 50 inches (127 cm)

HABITAT:
Deep ocean waters in the winter; shallow, warm coastal waters in the summer

CRUISING THE THAMES

In 1957, England's River Thames was declared "biologically dead." The 215-mile (346-km) river, which travels through London, was so polluted that it was believed it couldn't support wildlife. But in 2021, a "health check" revealed the river is very much alive—supporting everything from seahorses to eels to venomous sharks. Rising water temperatures and sewage still threaten the river's health, but spurdogs are cruising the waters.

VENOMOUS
COPYCATS
CAN YOU TELL THE DIFFERENCE?

JUST BECAUSE YOU AREN'T A VENOMOUS ANIMAL DOESN'T MEAN YOU CAN'T LOOK LIKE ONE. Some animals mimic, or copy, a venomous animal to protect themselves from predators. Clever!

COPY CAT

CORAL SNAKE OR SCARLET KING SNAKE?
With similar red, yellow, and black bands, spotting the difference between a coral snake and a scarlet king snake takes a careful eye. Here's a handy hint: If a red stripe is touching a yellow stripe, it's a coral snake. If a red stripe is touching a black stripe, it's a king snake. It's worth the second look: King snakes aren't venomous; however, while a bite from a coral snake might not initially hurt much, if victims aren't treated with antivenom, they will start having serious symptoms up to twelve hours later.

VENOMOUS

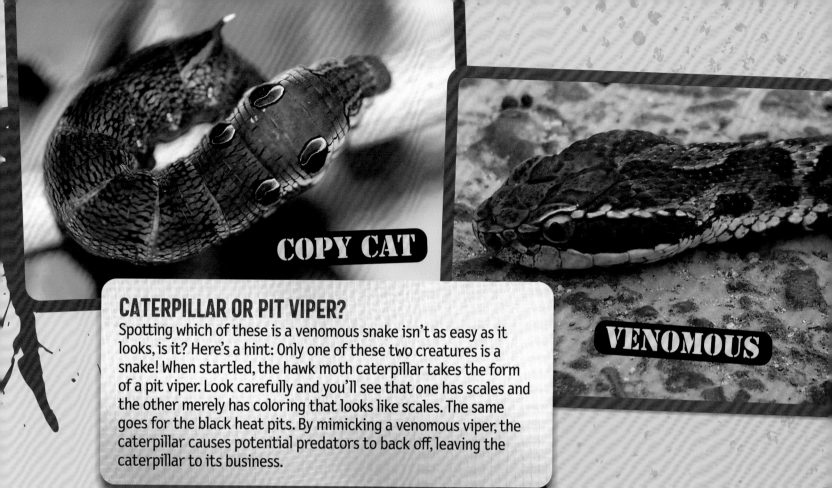

COPY CAT

VENOMOUS

CATERPILLAR OR PIT VIPER?
Spotting which of these is a venomous snake isn't as easy as it looks, is it? Here's a hint: Only one of these two creatures is a snake! When startled, the hawk moth caterpillar takes the form of a pit viper. Look carefully and you'll see that one has scales and the other merely has coloring that looks like scales. The same goes for the black heat pits. By mimicking a venomous viper, the caterpillar causes potential predators to back off, leaving the caterpillar to its business.

COPY CAT

VENOMOUS

MIMIC OCTOPUS OR SEA SNAKE?
How hard could it be to tell the difference between a snake and an octopus? After all, one has eight legs and the other has none. The mimic octopus is a pro at turning itself into something it's not. It is capable of mimicking a variety of animals—including a sole, a lionfish, and a highly venomous sea snake called a banded sea krait. The snake trick comes in especially handy: Damselfish are a favorite prey of banded sea kraits, but damselfish are territorial and willing to take on a mimic octopus. To defend itself, a mimic octopus hides by a rock and waves just one krait-looking arm out, which sends damselfish swimming.

DEADLY
MAMMALS

THESE VENOMOUS MAMMALS ARE LIKE NO OTHERS

THERE'S A VERY SHORT LIST OF MAMMALS THAT MAKE THE VENOMOUS LIST, AND THEY ARE ONE ODD SQUAD. Take the platypus: An otter-like creature with a nose like a duck and a spur on its heel like a cowboy, delivering venom with a painful poke to its rivals. Then there's the slow loris: Don't let those adorable wide eyes fool you. They keep predators away by covering themselves in toxins. And then there's the vampire bat: Let's just say it lives up to its name. Get ready to enter the wildly quirky world of venomous warm-blooded creatures.

A vampire bat can recognize the breathing patterns of **A SINGLE COW** and return to it night after night.

DUCK-BILLED PLATYPUS

SERIOUSLY FIERCE FEET

THERE MIGHT NOT BE ANY ANIMAL WEIRDER THAN THE PLATYPUS. It has traits that seem to draw from all areas of the animal kingdom: It's a mammal, but it lays eggs; it has a beaver-like tail, webbed feet, and a duck-like bill. The bill is covered in thousands of cells that pick up electrical signals given off by underwater animals. **THE FIRST SCIENTISTS WHO TOOK A LOOK AT A PLATYPUS WERE CONVINCED IT WAS A HOAX**—that surely this creature couldn't be real. Well, it is real, and it has some pretty impressive features—and one that's particularly stunning.

THE STING

If they weren't unique enough, male platypuses take it one step further: **THEY HAVE VENOMOUS SPURS ON THEIR HEELS!** When fighting or showing dominance, male platypuses can use their hind legs to poke competitors with their spurs, delivering venom.

Baby platypuses are the size of a **LIMA BEAN** when they're born.

💀 THE KILL

THE VENOM IS STRONG ENOUGH TO SEND COMPETITION SWIMMING OR RUNNING THE OTHER WAY. (Platypuses live in water and on land.) Humans are rarely stung by platypuses, but when they are, the pain can last for weeks. There is one positive side to their venom: **SCIENTISTS HAVE FOUND A HORMONE IN IT THAT THEY THINK COULD ONE DAY BE USED TO HELP PEOPLE WITH DIABETES.**

AT A GLANCE

SCIENTIFIC NAME:
Ornithorhynchus anatinus

SIZE:
Head and body: 15 inches (38 cm); tail: five inches (12.7 cm)

HABITAT:
Freshwater systems

A platypus can retract the **WEBBING ON ITS FEET,** exposing its nails so it can run on land.

VAMPIRE BAT

BLOODTHIRSTY AND VENOMOUS

BATS ARE THE ONLY MAMMAL THAT CAN FLY, AND VAMPIRE BATS ARE THE ONLY ONES THAT SURVIVE ON BLOOD. Venom helps them out in that process.

Most bats are harmless, but vampire bats—which live in Mexico, Central America, and South America—go for blood. Living in colonies of up to a thousand and often sleeping in caves, the bats emerge at night to **FEED ON THE BLOOD OF CATTLE AND HORSES.** But the animals aren't harmed—in fact, they usually don't even notice that the bats are biting.

Unlike other bats, which can only fly, vampire bats use their **FRONT AND HIND LIMBS** to run, walk, and hop on all fours.

THE BITE

VAMPIRE BATS HAVE A SPECIALIZED HEAT SENSOR ON THEIR NOSES that helps them find where blood is flowing under their victim's skin. Then they bite with their **EXTRA-SHARP TEETH AND DRAW OUT THEIR LONG TONGUES TO LAP UP THE BLOOD.**

Some bats **SPIT UP BLOOD** and share it with other bats in exchange for grooming.

☠ THE KILL

VENOM IN THE BATS' SALIVA HELPS PREVENT BLOOD FROM CLOTTING, ALLOWING THEM TO FEED FOR ABOUT 30 MINUTES. A vampire bat can eat its body weight in blood in just 20 minutes! Even though this doesn't affect the health of a cow, in one year, a 100-bat colony is **CAPABLE OF DRINKING THE BLOOD OF 25 COWS!**

AT A GLANCE

SCIENTIFIC NAME:
Desmodus rotundus

SIZE:
Body: 3.5 inches (9 cm);
wingspan: seven inches (18 cm)

HABITAT:
Tropics and subtropics

VENOM
SURVIVALISTS
WHO'S AFRAID OF A LITTLE SNAKE VENOM?

SHARP FANGS? VENOMOUS BITE? NO PROBLEM! A few animals are willing to tolerate a dose of venom if it means they can get dinner. Let's find out how they do it.

HONEY BADGER

You can't call a honey badger a picky eater. Up to 25 percent of its diet consists of venomous snakes. How is that possible? For starters, honey badgers have a big skull, long claws, and strong teeth, so they can hold their own when they attack. In addition, their skin is tough and loose—which means if anything tries to bite their necks, they can twist around and bite back. But their real superpower is a resistance to the venom of snakes and—as its name suggests—bees. Sure, a bite from certain venomous cobras and vipers can slow a honey badger down, but not for long. They can also withstand the stings of hundreds of bees, which is good, because honey badgers eat plenty of honey and bee larvae.

MONGOOSE

Cobras are fast and their bite means business, but certain species of mongooses are able to turn this slithery predator into prey. When a mongoose faces a cobra, it uses its speed to dart from side to side, avoiding a strike and countering with a powerful bite to the cobra's head. Occasionally a mongoose does get bitten, but no worries. They have evolved a venom resistance, and a bite doesn't faze them.

OPOSSUM

Opossums may be slow-moving and play dead at the first sign of trouble, but these marsupials are no slouches. First of all, "playing possum" often gets them out of sticky situations—animals often walk away from the seemingly dead opossum, allowing it to escape. But when faced with, say, a rattlesnake, opossums can rely on a more technical defense: venom resistance. Opossums have a special protein in their blood that neutralizes venom. Scientists are studying their blood in the hopes of one day producing better antivenoms that might save human lives.

SLOW LORIS

The Sunda slow loris has the **LONGEST TONGUE** of all primates— and uses it to drink nectar.

CUTE, FUZZY, AND DEADLY

With their giant round eyes and super soft fur, **SLOW LORISES DON'T EXACTLY LOOK LIKE VENOMOUS KILLERS,** but they are the only primate with the distinction of being venomous. These nocturnal animals live in trees in the forests of South and Southeast Asia, and they use their big eyes to see at night. **TO FIGHT OFF PREDATORS—LIKE SNAKES AND ORANGUTANS—THEY USE A SECRET WEAPON.**

 ## THE BITE

SLOW LORISES HAVE GLANDS UNDER THE CROOKS OF THEIR INNER ARMS THAT SECRETE TOXINS. During grooming, they spread the oily substance across their fur. This comes in handy when they're threatened: They curl into a ball that exposes their toxic fur, which predators steer clear of when they taste or smell it. Here's what makes slow lorises venomous: **THEY ALSO HAVE TOXINS IN THEIR SALIVA.** If they attack a predator by biting it, the venom is released into the wound.

☠ THE KILL

THE BITE FROM A SLOW LORIS CAN BE FATAL TO PREDATORS, but this critter has yet another unexpected self-defense trick that comes in handy. When threatened by predators, it will hiss and put its paws up over its head. Combined with dark facial markings, this position makes a slow loris look **LIKE THE EXPANDED HOOD OF A SPECTACLED COBRA,** tricking predators into thinking the slow loris is much more dangerous than it actually is.

Because of the size and structure of its eyes, a slow loris can see in almost **COMPLETE DARKNESS.**

AT A GLANCE

SCIENTIFIC NAME:
Nycticebus

SIZE:
8 to 12 inches (20 to 30 cm)

HABITAT:
Forests

VENOMOUS
WANNABES
NATURE'S PRICKLY VENOM BORROWERS

THESE ANIMALS DON'T MAKE THEIR OWN VENOM, but they still find ways to poke around with deadly toxins.

AFRICAN CRESTED RAT

The African crested rat has quill-like hair that can poke like a needle. But the rat doesn't produce its own toxin. While its pokes may be uncomfortable, they don't cause any serious damage. So what's a rat to do? Find a toxin.

The crested rat, which lives in East Africa, gnaws on the bark of *Acokanthera* trees, which contains a deadly toxin. With a mouthful of toxic bark, the rat drools on its own hair, which absorbs the toxin. Then, if a predator—such as a leopard, jackal, or wild dog—tries to eat the crested rat, it gets more than it bargained for. The toxin causes paralysis and, in high enough doses, a heart attack.

But the question that has scientists scratching their heads is, Why doesn't the tree toxin affect the rat? For now, scientists aren't sure, but they think it might have something to do with the makeup of the rat's saliva.

HEDGEHOG

Hedgehogs aren't venomous, but they hang around animals that have some toxins to spare. Hedgehogs are covered in about 5,000 spines, which serve as armor to protect their soft underbodies from predators such as badgers and weasels. Besides being a prickly deterrent, there's another way spines help make hedgehogs less than desirable to predators: Hedgehogs sometimes lick the toxins from toads, and then lick their own spines. With some luck, these toxins will cause an attacker to spit out a hedgehog rather than eat it.

SHREW

VENOMOUS CREATURES WITH A DARK SIDE

SHREWS ARE SEEMINGLY UNASSUMING LITTLE MAMMALS. Found all over the world—from North and South America to Africa and Eurasia—they are just a few inches long and survive mostly on insects. Sound innocent enough? Think again. **MANY SPECIES OF SHREWS ARE VENOMOUS, AND THEIR HUNTING METHOD IS A WEE BIT CREEPY.**

Shrews need to **EAT EVERY FEW HOURS.**

THE BITE

SHREWS HAVE GLANDS IN THEIR LOWER JAWS THAT PRODUCE VENOM, and when they bite into their prey, toxins are released into the wound.

THE KILL

A SHREW'S TOXIN DOESN'T KILL ITS PREY; IT PARALYZES IT. This is where it gets a little dark ... a shrew will stash its paralyzed—but still living—prey and then go on the hunt for more, **ACCUMULATING A PILE OF IMMOBILE SNACKS.** When it's hungry, it returns to its stash to feast. This is called "live hoarding."

A mealworm bitten by a shrew can be kept alive but **PARALYZED** for 15 days!

AT A GLANCE

SCIENTIFIC NAME:
Soricidae (family)

SIZE:
Two to three inches (6 to 8 cm)

HABITAT:
Found throughout the world, usually living in soil or moist environments

A SHREW WITH SUPER STRENGTH

With a name like "Thor's hero shrew," you can assume this creature has some serious strength. Thanks to unique interlocking vertebrae, the Thor's hero shrew is stronger—relative to its body mass—than any other animal with a spine. The shrew can withstand the weight of a full-grown Great Dane on its back. That's the equivalent of a human holding up the weight of a space shuttle!

TO THE RESCUE

WHEN A SNAKE BITES, VENOM ONE RESPONDS

THERE ARE A LOT OF SNAKES IN FLORIDA'S MIAMI-DADE COUNTY. In fact, you're up to eight times more likely to encounter a venomous water moccasin snake in neighborhoods there than you would in Everglades National Park. Luckily, there's the Venom Response Team, also known as Venom One.

Venom One is a special rescue team that helps people who have been bitten by venomous animals such as snakes, spiders, scorpions, or Africanized honey bees. Captain Jeffrey Fobb, a member of Venom One, brings antivenom to victims, identifies potentially venomous animals, and relocates the animals from people's homes.

Here is what Captain Fobb has learned during his 40 years handling venomous animals.

NATIONAL GEOGRAPHIC: What is the most common call that Venom One receives?

CAPTAIN FOBB: That people have seen or been bitten by a water moccasin snake. In South Florida there are a lot of new housing developments, building on what was part of the Everglades. The snakes are now concentrated in these areas, and people are living in close proximity to them.

NG: What should you do if you are bitten by a snake?

CAPTAIN FOBB: Call 911 if you're in the U.S., or your local emergency number, and follow the operator's instructions.

NG: Venom One delivers antivenom to bite victims. How does that work?

CAPTAIN FOBB: We maintain an antivenom bank with antivenom for all kinds of venomous animals, and get it to the victim. We also work with people to figure out the type of venomous animal that bit or stung them. If you get bit or stung by an animal, take a photo of it. You don't have to kill or capture it.

NG: How many calls does Venom One get every year?

CAPTAIN FOBB: As many as a hundred just for snakebites.

NG: Venom One also traps and relocates venomous animals that people find in their homes. Isn't that dangerous?

CAPTAIN FOBB: I don't find dealing with the animals that harrowing. We use snake hooks and tongs for special situations. There's a bagging device on the end of a pole. The rest is problem-solving. It keeps you on your toes and thinking.

NG: Have you ever been bitten by a snake?

CAPTAIN FOBB: Yes, but not a venomous one.

NG: How can people avoid being bitten by a venomous animal?

CAPTAIN FOBB: Look where you're putting your hands and feet. Be aware of your surroundings. We are living alongside wildlife. When it's inside our homes, that's inappropriate. When it's outside, that's where it lives. We are trying to help people coexist with animals.

ECHIDNA

THIS MAMMAL JUST LOST ITS VENOM STATUS

Despite being adorably prickly like a hedgehog and having a snout that resembles a shrew, **ECHIDNAS ARE MOST CLOSELY RELATED TO THE PLATYPUS.** Like platypuses, they are rare mammals that lay eggs. The male short-beaked echidna even has a spur on its heel like a platypus. **THAT SPUR ONCE GAVE ECHIDNAS VENOMOUS STATUS.** But recently, scientists took a closer look at the spur—and the substance that comes out over it—and their findings kicked echidnas off the list.

Look familiar? Baby echidnas and nifflers, the fictional creatures that like to steal shiny things in the *FANTASTIC BEASTS* films, are look-alikes.

THE STING

MILLIONS OF YEARS AGO, ECHIDNAS WERE VENOMOUS—they created venom just like platypuses and delivered it through their spurs. But over time, the venom wasn't really needed, and eventually the spurs took on a new role. Scientists discovered that **THE SUBSTANCE NOW RELEASED FROM THE SPURS IS USED BY ECHIDNAS TO COMMUNICATE WITH EACH OTHER.**

☠ THE KILL

Don't write off echidnas just yet, though. **THEY HAVE PLENTY OF UNIQUE QUALITIES TO MAKE UP FOR THEIR LACK OF VENOM.** For starters, they have special electroreceptors in the skin of their beaks that pick up on the movement of such prey as ants and termites. They also have long, sticky tongues that they use to pick up these insects, just like an anteater.

Baby echidnas are called **PUGGLES.**

AT A GLANCE
SCIENTIFIC NAME:
Tachyglossidae (family)

SIZE:
16 to 22 inches (40 to 55 cm)

HABITAT:
Forests, grasslands, deserts

CUBAN SOLENODON

THE SHYEST VENOMOUS MAMMAL

THE CUBAN SOLENODON APPEARS TO BE A MISHMASH OF CREATURES: It's the size of a guinea pig; it has a rat-like tail; it has a bendy, Pinocchio-like nose; and its **TEETH HAVE GROOVES IN THEM THAT ARE USED TO INJECT VENOM** into its prey, like a snake.

Solenodons **SMELL LIKE GOATS!** They have glands in their armpits that secrete a goat-like odor.

 **THE BITE**

The end of a Cuban solenodon's nose has a ball-and-socket joint (like a human's hip), which means it's super flexible. This allows it to root around in dirt, looking for insects, worms, snails, and even small reptiles. **THEN IT BITES THE PREY, DELIVERING A TOXIN THAT IMMOBILIZES THEM.**

When threatened, solenodons GRUNT LIKE PIGS.

☠ THE KILL

RELEASING A VENOM THAT CAUSES ITS VICTIM TO STOP IN ITS TRACKS comes in handy for an animal that has poor eyesight and would have trouble keeping track of prey trying to wriggle away. A solenodon's toxin is quick to take hold, causing paralysis and difficulty breathing. And for that reason, this animal that doesn't look like much of a threat can occasionally take on larger prey and get away with it. One solenodon that was in captivity in London attacked and ate a chicken!

AT A GLANCE

SCIENTIFIC NAME:
Solenodon cubanus

SIZE:
11 to 15 inches (28 to 38 cm)

HABITAT:
Caves and burrows in wet forests

LOST AND FOUND

The Cuban solenodon is so elusive that scientists thought it was extinct! Cuban solenodons are called "living fossils" because they haven't changed much over the course of millions of years. Now they face a serious threat of extinction. In the 19th century, deforestation in Cuba, the only place they live, cut their populations so quickly that scientists thought they had died out. Then, in the early 2000s, a few more were spotted. Today, the venomous shrew-like mammal hangs out in wet mountain forests of Cuba and still faces serious threats to its survival.

SO WEIRD

IT HAS TO BE TRUE

THERE'S MORE THAN ONE WAY TO BE WILD

SOME VENOMOUS MAMMALS AREN'T JUST FEARSOME—they're downright wacky, too. These unusual animals have talents that go beyond toxins. Just check out these bizarre behaviors.

PLATYPUSES CHEW WITH ROCKS.

A platypus has to eat 20 percent of its body weight each day to keep its energy up. But platypuses don't have teeth, so they scoop up tiny bits of gravel and dirt off the bottoms of rivers, streams, and lakes to help mash up their food before swallowing it.

BABY SHREWS MAKE A CONGA LINE.

Sometimes a shrew mama needs to make a quick escape to avoid danger, and other times she just needs to find a new hangout. To make sure no one gets lost, baby shrews, which are nearly blind, sometimes form a chain behind their mom, each grasping the base of the tail of the sibling in front of them with their mouth. It looks a bit like a conga line! This mode of transport for shrews is called caravanning.

SLOW LORISES SLITHER LIKE SNAKES.

Not only do slow lorises mimic the look of a cobra, they copy its moves, too. Extra bones in their spines help them slither and twist like the snake.

SHREWS CAN WALK ON WATER.

Well, one kind of shrew can. The water shrew, which lives in the northern United States and Canada, dives and swims in water to look for food—and some have been seen walking on the surface of water! How do they do it? Scientists think they trap air bubbles on the hairs of their feet, allowing them to stay on the surface.

CREDITS

Credit Abbreviations: AS: Adobe Stock; ASP: Alamy Stock Photo; GI: Getty Images; ISP: iStock Photo; MP: Minden Pictures; NGIC: National Geographic Image Collection; SS: Shutterstock

Cover (background), Igor Vitkovskiy/SS; (bees), Daniel Prudek/SS; (bats), faiza/AS; (scorpion), Eric Isselée/AS; (splatter), MoonRock/SS; (loris), Charoenchai/AS; (snake), mgkuijpers/AS; back cover (UP), Mark MacEwen/Nature Picture Library; 1 (CTR), Mark Kostich/AS; 4 (UP LE), Tallies/SS; 4 (LO RT), Ernie Cooper/AS; 5 (UP LE), Alekss/AS; 5 (UP RT), Pete Waters/AS; 5 (CTR), Subaqueosshutterbug/ISP; 6 (CTR), Christian Vinces/SS; 7 (UP LE), Brendan Louw/AS; 7 (UP RT), Eric Isselée/AS; 7 (CTR), Ilya Akinshin/AS; 7 (LO RT), Firman Wahyudin/SS; 8 (LO LE), fivespots/SS; 9 (CTR), Shoemcfly/ISP; 10-11 (CTR), NickEvansKZN/SS; 10 (LO LE), mgkuijpers/AS; 11 (CTR RT), Maik Dobiey/Avalon; 12-13 (CTR), Uryadnikov Sergey/AS; 12 (LO LE), Uryadnikov Sergey/SS; 13 (CTR RT), Uryadnikov Sergey/AS; 13 (LO LE), Michael Dunning/GI; 14-15 (CTR), Opayaza12/SS; 14 (LO RT), dwi/AS; 15 (CTR RT), DS light photography /AS; 15 (LO LE), Mufti Adi/AS; 16-17 (UP CTR), mgkuijpers/AS; 17 (CTR RT), Maria Dryfhout/SS; 17 (LO), ondreicka/AS; 18-19 (CTR), Daniel Heuclin/Biosphoto; 18 (LO LE), Jupiterimages/GI; 19 (CTR RT), Daniel Heuclin/Biosphoto; 20-21 (CTR), Tomasz/AS; 20 (LO RT), Suriya99/SS; 21 (CTR RT), Stalk/SS; 23-24 (UP LE), mgkuijpers/AS; 23 (LO LE), Daniel Heuclin/Avalon; 23 (LO RT), Eugene Troskie/SS; 24-25 (CTR), Kris/AS; 25 (UP RT), Neil Harrison/DT; 25 (LO RT), Joe McDonald/GI; 26-27 (CTR), NickEvansKZN/SS; 26 (LO LE), Johan Marais, African Snakebite Institute; 28-29 (CTR), Pirita/SS; 28 (LO LE), Narupon/AS; 29 (UP RT), zilvergolf/AS; 29 (LO RT), Mike Greenslade/Australia/ASP; 30-31 (CTR), Robert Valentic/Nature Picture Library; 31 (LO RT), Pakhnyushchyy/AS; 32-33 (CTR), Mark Higgins/SS; 32 (LO LE), mgkuijpers/AS; 33 (UP RT), Keith Rangko/AS; 33 (LO RT), Catherinelprod Catherine/DT; 34 (LO LE), Protasov AN/SS; 35 (CTR), Ernie Cooper/AS; 36-37 (CTR), Daniel Prudek/AS; 36 (LO LE), Ihor Sulyatytskyy/SS; 37 (CTR RT), Sketchart/SS; 37 (LO LE), StockMediaProduction/SS; 38-39 (UP LE), Michael Smith; 39 (CTR RT), mirkograul/AS; 39 (LO LE), Michael Smith; 40-41 (CTR), Ken Griffiths/SS; 40 (LO LE), Ken Griffiths/SS; 41 (UP RT), Elias/AS; 42-43 (UP CTR), Willem Van Zyl/AS; 42 (LO RT), Veronique Duplain/SS; 43 (LO RT), Fotos 593/AS; 44-45 (CTR), ondreicka/AS; 44 (LO LE), David Huntley Creative/SS; 45 (CTR RT), Pong Wira/SS; 46-47 (UP CTR), jbrown/AS; 46 (LO LE), Piotr Naskrecki/Minden; 47 (LO LE), Danny/AS; 47 (LO RT), nechaevkon/AS; 48-49 (CTR), Irina K./AS; 48 (LO LE), Ivan Kuzmin/AS; 49 (CTR RT), Mr.Aphirak Arkasamnuai/SS; 50 (LO RT), jiade/SS; 51 (UP CTR), DonyaHHI/SS; 51 (UP RT), Ken/AS; 51 (CTR), Chris/AS; 51 (CTR RT), Ken Griffiths/SS; 51 (LO LE), MIA Studio/SS; 52-53 (CTR), khlungcenter/SS; 52 (LO LE), Piman Khrutmuang/AS; 53 (LO LE), MIA Studio/SS; 54 (LO LE), Carlos Jared; 55 (UP LE), Cornel Constantin/SS; 55 (CTR RT), Simon Richards; 55 (LO LE), mgkuijpers/AS; 56-57 (CTR), ciclopata/AS; 56 (LO LE), Dan Olsen/SS; 57 (LO RT), Sun4k/SS; 58-59 (CTR), Svetlana67/SS; 58 (LO LE), Milan Zygmunt/SS; 59 (UP RT), Samuel/AS; 59 (CTR RT), Chase D'animulls/SS; 60 (LO LE), bluehand/AS; 61 (CTR), elena_photo_soul/SS; 62-63 (CTR), Thomas P. Peschak/NGIC; 62 (LO LE), Dewald Kirsten/SS; 63 (CTR RT), Bangtalay/SS; 63 (LO LE), Olivia Zhou/AS; 64-65 (UP CTR), Ken Griffiths/SS; 64 (LO RT), Peter/AS; 65 (CTR RT), Saurav Karki/ASP; 65 (LO LE), Holger T.K./AS; 66-67 (CTR), aapsky/AS; 66 (LO LE), Mark Kostich/ISP; 67 (CTR RT), Adam/AS; 67 (LO LE), World History Archive/ASP; 68-69 (CTR), Massimo Rudoni/SS; 68 (LO LE), Oksana/AS; 69 (CTR RT), Paulo de Oliveira/Minden; 70 (LO), DS light photography/AS; 71 (UP RT), torook/AS; 71 (CTR LE), Tammy616/ISP; 71 (LO RT), mgkuijpers/AS; 72-73 (CTR), Yusran Abdul Rahman/SS; 72 (LO LE), K.Pock Pics/SS; 73 (CTR RT), Brent Durand/GI; 74 (LO), reptiles4all/SS; 75 (UP LE), bearacreative/AS; 75 (CTR RT), Franny Constantina/SS; 75 (LO LE), bayazed/AS; 76-77 (CTR), Jenny Lord/SS; 76 (CTR), Andy/AS; 77 (CTR RT), DiveSpin/SS; 78-79 (CTR), Hannah SM/AS; 78 (LO LE), Andrea Izzotti/AS; 79 (UP RT), Kyle Lippenberger/SS; 79 (LO LE), uwimages/AS; 80-81 (CTR), Andy Murch/Nature Picture Library; 80 (LO LE), Anion/AS; 81 (CTR RT), Joem/AS; 81 (LO LE), Leonid Andronov/AS; 82 (CTR LE), erllre/AS; 82 (LO CTR), luisrock6299/AS; 83 (UP LE), Eileen Kumpf/SS; 83 (UP RT), JoshuaDaniel/SS; 83 (LO LE), ead72/AS; 83 (LO RT), Richard Carey/AS; 84 (LO LE), denboma/AS; 85 (CTR), belizar/AS; 86 (LO LE), slowmotiongli/AS; 87-86 (CTR), 169169/AS; 87 (CTR RT), 169169/AS; 88-89 (CTR), Geza Farkas/AS; 88 (LO LE), Michael Lynch/SS; 89 (CTR RT), Oxford Scientific/GI; 90 (LO), Erwin Niemand/SS; 91 (UP), Gallo Images-Dave Hamman/GI; 91 (LO), Kassia Marie Ott/SS; 92-93 (CTR), Conservationist/SS; 92 (LO LE), Charoenchai/AS; 93 (CTR RT), seregraff/AS; 94 (LO), Sara Weinstein; 95 (CTR), DenisNata/AS; 96-95 (CTR), Wirestock/AS; 96 (LO), creativenature.nl/AS; 97 (CTR RT), Less/AS; 97 (LO LE), Madhava Meegaskumbura; 99 (UP), Jeffrey Fobb; 100-101 (CTR), Jarrod Calati/ISP; 100 (LO LE), Ken Griffiths/SS; 101 (CTR RT), tracielouise/ISP; 102-103 (CTR), Eladio Fernandez/Caribbean Nature Photography.; 102 (LO LE), Joel Sartore/NGIC; 103 (CTR RT), Joel Sartore/NGIC; 103 (LO LE), Joel Sartore/NGIC; 104 (LO), PIXATERRA/AS; 105 (UP LE), reativenature.nl/AS; 105 (CTR RT), Emi/AS; 105 (LO LE), Warmer/SS; 106 (UP LE), Henk/AS; 106 (LO RT), adogslifephoto/AS; 107, kikkerdirk/AS; 108, Sharon Keating/AS; 109, abet/AS; 110, Eric Isselée/AS; 111, bennytrapp/AS; 112, Uryadnikov Sergey/AS

INDEX

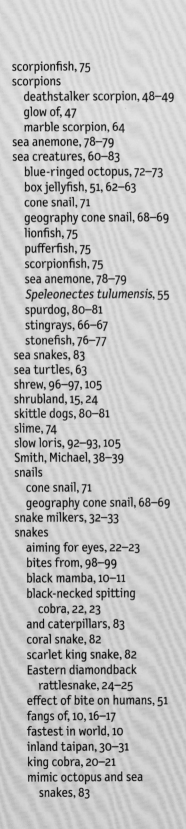

Since 1888, the National Geographic Society has funded more than 14,000 research, conservation, education, and storytelling projects around the world. National Geographic Partners distributes a portion of the funds it receives from your purchase to National Geographic Society to support programs including the conservation of animals and their habitats. To learn more, visit natgeo.com/info.

For more information, visit nationalgeographic.com, call 1-877-873-6846, or write to the following address:

National Geographic Partners, LLC
1145 17th Street NW
Washington, DC 20036-4688 U.S.A.

For librarians and teachers: nationalgeographic.com/books/librarians-and-educators

More for kids from National Geographic: natgeokids.com

National Geographic Kids magazine inspires children to explore their world with fun yet educational articles on animals, science, nature, and more. Using fresh storytelling and amazing photography, Nat Geo Kids shows kids ages 6 to 14 the fascinating truth about the world—and why they should care. **natgeo.com/subscribe**

For rights or permissions inquiries, please contact National Geographic Books Subsidiary Rights: bookrights@natgeo.com

Designed by Waterbury Publications, Inc., Des Moines, IA.

Library of Congress Cataloging-in-Publication Data

Names: Beer, Julie, author.
Title: Bite, sting, kill / Julie Beer.
Description: Washington, D.C. : National Geographic Kids, 2023. | Audience: Ages 8-12 | Audience: Grades 4-6
Identifiers: LCCN 2021035987 | ISBN 9781426373411 (hardcover) | ISBN 9781426373909 (library binding)
Subjects: LCSH: Poisonous animals--Juvenile literature.
Classification: LCC QL100 .B44 2023 | DDC 591.6/5--dc23
LC record available at https://lccn.loc.gov/2021035987

ACKNOWLEDGMENTS
The publisher wishes to thank the Waterbury Publications team: Lisa Kingsley, editorial director; Ken Carlson, creative director; Doug Samuelson, associate art director; and Tricia Bergman, associate editor; and the National Geographic Kids team: Shelby Lees, senior editor; Brett Challos, art director; Sarah J. Mock, senior photo editor; and Anne LeongSon and Gus Tello, design associates.

Printed in China
22/RRDH/1